HOW TO GET A JOB IN TELEVISION

SECOND EDITION

SUSAN WALLS

howtobooks

Published by How To Books Ltd,
3 Newtec Place, Magdalen Road,
Oxford OX4 1RE, United Kingdom.
Tel: (01865) 793806. Fax: (01865) 248780.
Email: info@howtobooks.co.uk
http://www.howtobooks.co.uk

First edition 2002
Second edition 2006

Susan Walls has asserted the right to be identified as the author of this
work, in accordance with the Copyright, Designs and Patents Act 1988.

British Library Cataloguing in Publication Data.
A catalogue record for this book is available from
the British Library.

Produced for How To Books by Deer Park Productions, Tavistock
Typeset by Kestrel Data, Exeter, Devon
Cover design by Baseline Arts Ltd, Oxford
Printed and bound by Cromwell Press Ltd, Trowbridge, Wiltshire

NOTE: The material contained in this book is set out in good
faith for general guidance and no liability can be accepted
for loss or expense incurred as a result of relying in particular
circumstances on statements made in the book. Laws and
regulations are complex and liable to change, and readers should
check the current position with the relevant authorities before
making personal arrangements.

HOW TO GET A JOB IN TELEVISION

If you want to know how . . .

Getting into Films and Television
'Explains what everybody does in the film industry, and helps the reader aim at the right job.' – *The Times*

'A really useful guide to the subject . . .' – *The Daily Telegraph*

Successful Interviews Every Time
' . . . clearly written and to the point. To be interviewed without having read it is an opportunity missed.' – *The Sunday Times*

'It helped me to secure the job I wanted at the salary I wanted.' – C. Hussey

Turn Your Degree into a Career
A step-by-step guide to achieving your dream career

'. . . offers a comprehensive range of advice; from finding out what you're good at, developing a career strategy and managing your motivation through to getting the job you want.' – Broadview

howtobooks

For full details, please send for a free copy
of the latest catalogue to:

How To Books
3 Newtec Place, Magdalen Road
Oxford OX4 1RE, United Kingdom
email: info@howtobooks.co.uk
www.howtobooks.co.uk

Contents

So You Want to Work in TV: Why You Should Read this Book

I have loved being a television researcher. It's the best job in the world: sometimes exhausting, often frustrating, but always, always fascinating. I've interviewed war heroes, foreign leaders and striking miners. I've been to teenage Supermodel school, and I've met the guy who invented mountain bikes, up a mountain in California. I've spent a day in Hollywood with the movie-trailer-voice-over-man, and I've flown in a First World War biplane. I have home contact numbers for brilliant scientists, Hollywood stuntmen, and some of the world's most beautiful people. Dannii Minogue has worn my bikini.

I wrote this book because I felt there was a need for it – three needs, in fact.

The first was the need to explain what working in television is really like – the good bits and the bad. Lots of books will teach you how to do research, but they won't tell you how to *be* a researcher. Plenty of technical manuals will show you how to frame a shot or pull focus, but they won't prepare you for what it's like to work as part of a crew.

I've been doing this job for 20 years now, and I'm still learning, because there's so much to learn. And I'm not just talking about understanding the nuts and bolts of pro-gramme-making. In some ways, that's the easy bit. The tricky skills to master are the people skills – how to get people involved with the project, how to treat interviewees and artists, and how to deal with the rest of the team: crew, directors, presenters, actors, editors, and everyone else that you need to get along with. Because that's the secret of getting on in television – knowing how to get on with people.

The second reason for writing this book was to help you find the TV job that's best for you. Unless you know where you're heading, you'll be rejected on the spot when you write your first can-I-have-a-job letter. TV bosses get too many letters that start 'I want to work in television, and I'll do anything'. These sort of letters make the writer sound desperate, as well as sadly misinformed about the television industry. Every television job is specialised – if you think that being a researcher is just like being a floor manager or an editor, then you are so far off the mark that you need to read this book today, this moment. It's imperative that you find out what you want to do *before* you start applying for jobs.

The third and most important reason for writing this book was to encourage the right sort of people to come into television. This might surprise you – isn't there a glut of applicants for every job in British TV? Sure, but most of them want to be in television for all the wrong reasons (glamour, status, money) and are therefore entirely unsuited to a future in making programmes.

Television doesn't need people who are interested in television. It needs people who are interested in the world and how it works: people who want to share knowledge and ideas and tell exciting stories. It needs people with energy and enthusiasm, vision and vigour, a sense of humour, and the sense to spot a good story. Because telling stories is what television is all about, no matter what job you decide you want to do.

A friend of mine heads a department at a major network company. He's constantly on the look-out for new talent, and constantly disappointed by the kind of people who apply. Rarely, someone bright and interesting comes along, dazzling him with their passion and enthusiasm, and it cheers him up for weeks. More often than not, though, he has to deal with applicants who are stuffy, self-important, or downright dull. Here's a secret – there are not enough good people to go round. TV needs more people with passion.

Once you've read this book, you could be the next Bright Young Thing in British Television. I can't promise you that it will bring you great riches, but I can guarantee you adventure and excitement, a job worth getting up for in the morning, and some fascinating tales to tell your friends.

Susan Walls

Preface
to Second edition

Things change fast in television, and there's an awful lot of change around at the moment.

Just a few years ago, ITV was a federation of medium-sized companies. Now it's nearly completed the move to become one big one. Inevitably, this evolution is having an impact on training and job opportunities. Meanwhile, Channel 4 and the BBC are vying to increase their share of the 'TV multiverse' by setting up new channels to broadcast their old programmes. But at the same time, the corporation is shedding staff jobs – which is bad news for BBC staffers, but good news for independent producers.

Television programmes are changing too: they're becoming increasingly polarised between low-budget, home-grown shows, and high-end, expensive co-productions made for transmission in several countries. The 'medium-sized' shows – the kind of programmes that used to be part of the learning curve for trainees – are slowly but inexorably disappearing from the schedules.

Production technology is also undergoing a revolution. The fully-digital newsroom is now a reality in many regional TV stations – so no more jobs for news VT editors, but lots of exciting opportunities for the new breed of journalist/presenter/picture editors who are trained to produce their own stories, from beginning to end. (The good VT editors, of course, will move on to the high-end, big-budget, international co-productions).

But in all this upheaval, one thing hasn't changed. TV bosses are still looking for the same kind of people – people with passion, ideas and enthusiasm. People like you.

This revised and expanded edition of How To Get a Job in Television tells you how to use these industry changes to your advantage, and get your first foothold in the exciting and satisfying world of television production.

Acknowledgements

As always on a project, lots of people helped. Programme makers: Ian Cundall; Andrew Hill; Dee Marshall; Stephen Haggard; Dave Selwood; Adam Severs; Helen Scott; Matthew Rook; Neil Shand; Alison Turner; Tim Wybrow; Sheila Fitzhugh; Barbara Govan; Anna Kost; Mark Witty; Paul Bader; Richard Maude; Nick Gray; Graeme Pollard; John Smith. Managers, trainers and recruiters: Emma Clifford; Robert Alcock; Liz Westbrook; Lance Tattershall; Sue Clark; Sara Harrison; Karen Illingworth; Terry Mounsey; James Mackie; Cherry Ehrlich; Neil Walker; Steve Jenkinson. Health and Safety experts: Jane Curtis; Alice Holden. Regulator: Isobel Reid. Educators: Chris Wensley; Paul Inman; Diane Dalziel; Fiona Thompson; Kate Mulhoy.

Thanks to you all, and apologies to anyone I inadvertently left out. Any mistakes are mine.

And finally, special thanks to my husband, Patrick, for everything: for helping with the research and writing, for proof-reading the manuscript, and for sharing his twenty-five years of experience.

Author's Note

Four things to note:

- ◆ I've used the pronouns 'he' and 'she' indiscriminately and interchangeably.

- ◆ Some names have been changed, to protect people who told me stories, but got shy about seeing them in print.

- ◆ I've cheerfully broken old-fashioned rules of grammar and syntax. That's because this book is written in the style of a television script, and TV writing should sound like everyday speech. So please don't write and complain that I split an infinitive or ended a sentence with a preposition – that's how people talk.

- ◆ Most introduction-to-TV books have a list of useful addresses. This one doesn't, because TV companies are changing so fast that any such list would be out of date within a year. The industry training organisation Skillset, and its sister organisation Skillsformedia, have excellent websites – use them to put together your own list of useful addresses!

Part 1
Welcome to Television

'There are a million jobs in television; working out which one you want to do is the first step towards being successful.'

Steven Andrew, Contoller of Off Peak, ITV

1

The Story of a Shoot

Before we go any further, here's a story to inspire you, and perhaps to warn you. It's the true tale of a week-long foreign shoot for a teenage show for ITV. The programme is a BAFTA-winning factual series called The Scoop. The budget is tight, but production values are high. In other words, it's an ordinary week's filming for an ordinary programme – this is how you make television. If you can't work at this pace, then forget television as a career choice. Budgets get smaller every year, and the only way producers can still make programmes is by packing more work into every day.

On each Scoop shoot, there are two production people: a senior researcher or a producer, and a director. There's also a crew of two (camera and sound), and a presenter (for this shoot, it's Australian actress Isla Fisher).

FRIDAY 1 MAY

09.30, Room 806, Parc St Charles Hotel, New Orleans

Script meeting with Patrick the director. Just a few hours to go before the others arrive; we start shooting tomorrow. Spend the morning going over the shooting schedules and scripts for the six days' filming ahead – we shoot, on average, enough material for one five-minute story per day.

We've been in New Orleans for five days, doing 'recces', which means checking out the locations and the stories that I set up on the phone from England. Nothing is quite as we expected: some of the stories are better than we hoped, and some are not so good. But all of them need a re-think. So we've been re-working the scripts as we go along – sometimes late into the night. Now we have six strong scripts, and just time enough to put in those little touches that make a good story great.

By the time the rest of the team arrive, the shoot should be planned like a military campaign. We need to produce clear directions to all the locations, with maps and instructions on where to park. We also need detailed shooting schedules – giving breakdowns of every shot and piece of action, and where it takes place – because the stories will be shot out of order, in several locations.

Here are the stories:

◆ The ritual of the American high school prom.

◆ The technology behind the biggest indoor sports arena in the world, the New Orleans Superdome.

◆ How the invention of poker changed the look of playing cards, and added new riches to the English language.

◆ The roots of rock: why New Orleans was the birthplace of pop music.

◆ The amazing skills of the rodeo families of Louisiana.

◆ The strange story of the only white alligators in the world.

Late afternoon we pick up our presenter from New Orleans airport. Isla Fisher's enthusiasm for the city and the stories and the sunshine and anything else she can think of lifts our jaded spirits. Suddenly, we're looking forward to this shoot. I help Isla unpack. She's exhausted from her flight, so I iron her clothes and order her some food. (I'm in charge of the presenter, which is fine by me because Isla is a peach and a treat to work with. But some 'talents' are hell on earth, and you'll feel more like strangling them than ordering them room service.)

While I look after Isla, the director goes to the airport to greet the crew, and help them organise a hired van for the shoot. The lighting cameraman Matthew and sound recordist Tim have been travelling for 18 hours with 13 heavy flight cases. These kinds of shoots used to be crewed by three technicians – camera, sound and a spark – but cuts got made, and now the camera operator has to carry all the lighting gear, as well as all the camera equipment. So Matt and Tim are tired. Very, very tired. But when they finally get to the hotel, they have to get out all the kit and check that it survived the journey. Everyone thinks that baggage-handlers chuck their stuff around. Matt knows it. He's turned up in foreign parts before with a camera that's in three pieces. Seems the baggage-manglers are not much impressed by the big yellow FRAGILE stickers on the side of flight cases.

Later we meet for a light supper, a production meeting, and just the right amount of alcohol to calm our nerves.

Sometimes, just thinking about how much work you have to do is harder than actually doing it.

SATURDAY 2 MAY

08.00, Parc St Charles Hotel
Day one of the shoot – it's magic time! We're working until midnight tonight, filming at the high school prom, so it's a late start for the crew and presenter, but not for production. We've got costumes to hire: a Southern Belle dress for Isla, and a Tuxedo for Tim-the-sound-recordist, who's going to be her on-camera prom date. (Well, we thought it was funny!)

12.00, Bourbon Street
The shoot starts for real. First we grab a PTC (piece to camera) from Isla in Bourbon Street for the story about the roots of rock. We don't have a filming permit for this, so it's done very quickly, with one eye out for police cars, and the other on the drunk guy who wants to marry Isla. (See Chapter 8 for information on filming permits.) Next, we stop off at the New Orleans Historical Society to get tape of archive photographs and drawings that we need to illustrate the poker story. The people at the society are wonderful, but very laid back, which makes us nervous – we have little time for small-talk. By the time we leave, we're already behind schedule. On the way to the next location, we pick up a 'beauty shot' of the port of New Orleans, which we also need for the poker story. This one shot takes 20 minutes to shoot,

and another half-an-hour to get to the place where we need to shoot it (over on the opposite bank of the Mississippi), but it's worth it because it adds richness to the story. This is what the phrase 'high production values' means. We grab some sandwiches for lunch, and eat them in the van.

15.30, A beauty parlour deep in the suburbs of New Orleans

The girl we've chosen to follow to the prom tonight is getting her hair and makeup done, along with her best girlfriend. Isla gets made-up too, and does some funny impromptu PTCs as she gets the New Orleans 'prom look' makeover (think overkill: great coils of piled-up hair and country-singer makeup). Because this is a 'just-keep-rolling-and-let's-see-what-happens' bit of the story, the crew have to shoot everything, otherwise they'll miss one of Isla's remarks. Which means that I have to log hours of material. It's part of my job to take notes on every shot, so we can edit efficiently. There's no point shooting good material if you can't find it again later, so accurate notes are invaluable (more about this later, in Chapter 6). It's also my job to keep an eye on the schedule, to organise the next set-up for the director (so there's never any delay), and to keep everyone supplied with drinks as they work (there's rarely time for coffee-breaks on a shoot like this, even though the crew nag for one, pretty much all the time – it's part of their job description).

17.30, Still at the beauty parlour:

The 'make-overs' have taken longer than promised, and the director is getting grumpy. The girls look quite astonishing in their prom makeup and hair, like 50-year old extras from a pantomime.

The prom queens drive home to finish their transformations. We follow them, and set up to film in the house. We've arranged all this in advance, of course. The girl we've chosen to follow is called Jenine, and she's lucid about the importance of the prom as a rite of passage into adulthood for American teenagers. At least she was on the phone – in front of the camera, she whoops and giggles a lot and sprays glitter all over the cameraman.

Our angle on this story is the astounding amount of money these 17- and 18-year olds splash out on their prom: the hair, makeup, corsages, new dresses and hired suits, limos and pre-prom dinners, can add up to over a thousand dollars.

18.30, Jenine's house

The girls' dates turn up late, looking like bouncers from a sleezy nightclub, and we film them as they step grandly from their hired limo in their hired white suits – in fact we film them several times, as they keep laughing and spoiling the shot, and this puts us even further behind schedule. Next, we ask these two testosterone-soaked, probably slightly drunk teenage boys, to do some serious acting. The director wants to get a shot of them opening the door to Jenine's house, and smiling on cue, so he can put a 'ting' starburst on their teeth in post-production. This takes another half-hour, and much hilarity ensues. Honestly, you'd think these boys were here to have fun. Then we follow them into the house and catch their reactions as they see what the girls have done to themselves (they seem suitably impressed, but it's hard to tell with Americans).

There's much kissing and cheering and picture-taking by the assembled parents. (Annoyingly, they do all this kissing and cheering in a particularly dark part of the room, away from the area where Matthew has carefully placed his lights.) Then the boys whisk their dates off to a relaxed meal. We, on the other hand, have less than an hour to record one more PTC from Isla at the house, extract ourselves from the clutches of the weeping parents (who seem to think we're kindred spirits because we shared this moment with them – now they want to relive it endlessly!), then pack up all our gear, grab some food somewhere, and travel across to the other side of New Orleans to the hall where the prom is being held.

20.30, The prom party

We set up camp in the party room which is darker than anticipated. In fact it's almost black, with small pools of light (see Chapter 6, The Shoot: things to check on a recce). I can just about make out the cameraman's face, and he looks worried. This is what's known in the trade as a 'bad lighting situation'. But no time to worry – first we have to dash outside to get some shots of limos and horse-drawn carriages arriving. Except we can't find the way out of the massive building where the prom is being held. I recced the entrance, and where we should park our crew van, but I forgot to recce the exits. So we spend ages going round in circles, and up and down echoey corridors. We miss most of the limos, and we lose a lot of time. This is bad because we have a lot to shoot tonight, under difficult conditions: eccentric lighting, throbbing music, and hoards of aggressive prom-goers, who, we've just discovered, don't want us mucking up the most important day of their lives. Now this, I certainly hadn't anticipated. The teachers who organised the prom assured me that the students would be 'thrilled and honoured' to be filmed for British Television. In fact, they look murderous. I don't think that the teachers explained about us needing to turn off the music so we can record pieces from Isla . . .

23.30, Still at the prom

Isla has been threatened with a good beating by jealous girls who don't like the fact that she's so beautiful, and I've been jostled and jeered for turning off the music. All of us are tired, sweaty and half-deaf from the noise. But we've got some quite good material, and at last, we've finished shooting for the day – just 15½ hours after I started work this morning; 13½ hours after the crew clocked on.

00.10, Back at the Parc St Charles Hotel

We retire to the director's room for the obligatory how-was-the-first-day-of-the-shoot-for-you conversation over many, many beers. Everyone agrees it could have been much worse, which is encouraging.

SUNDAY 3 MAY

Day off

Spend the morning marking up my script (see Chapter 6 for notes on how to mark up a script), and the rest of the time worrying about the next five days. The crew go to a Doobie Brothers concert at the New Orleans Music Festival. They know how to live . . .

MONDAY 4 MAY

08.30, Parc St Charles Hotel lobby

Second day of shooting. Compared to Saturday, today should be a picnic, although Isla isn't looking forward to this morning, when we're shooting at the prom school. She hopes she won't be killed, and cheers up when she sees the 'NO GUNS OR DRUGS ALLOWED' sign outside school – at least she won't be shot by a drug-crazed prommer. Amazingly, the horrors of Saturday have melted away, and it seems that every student in the school truly is 'thrilled and honoured' to have us filming. Everyone's funny and welcoming, and we get some great stuff to set up the story, including some action shots of Jenine wrestling (she's the school champion!).

We even have time for a proper lunch, before heading back off into the centre of New Orleans to shoot at the world's largest indoor sports arena: the Louisiana Superdome. The dome can be turned into a venue for any event, and today its main floor is becoming an ice-rink for an ice dance extravaganza, organised by one of America's biggest entertainment companies. We are filming the transformation of the dome's main floor – or we should be – as part of our story on the building's technology. But, as ever when you're dealing with enormous organisations, things start to go wrong. It's a rule of the universe: the bigger the corporation, the less chance you have of getting access to whatever it is you want to film. Your request will go up and up the chain of command, and then mysteriously disappear. You will think you have every base covered, but they will have forgotten all about you.

So, we are due to do a piece from Isla with ice-laying going on in the background at 14.15, according to our schedule (which we've cleared with just about everyone in the building, including the on-site representative of the entertainment company). We get to the spot at 14.18, set up and . . . the ice-laying crew down tools and go for a lunchbreak. The foreman says they'll be back in about three hours' time, but they're behind schedule too, so he doesn't want us to do the shot then either.

18.30, Change location

We move next door to the Hyatt Hotel, whose roof offers the best view in town of the dome's glorious exterior. This one, three-second shot took quite a few phone calls to set up, and meant organising special parking for the crew, but the story wouldn't work without it. We need Isla in the shot, so we can see how tiny she looks beside the massive dome. The crew set off to the Hyatt's roof, while I stay with Isla, and prepare to stage-manage her into the right position once the crew are in place. The walkie-talkie crackles into life – it's Matthew, the cameraman, sounding businesslike: 'Go left 20 paces, now forward five, no, back a bit . . . actually maybe right a bit, that's good, we're getting there, just come forward a touch . . .' This nonsense goes on for at least ten minutes before I twig that the crew are still in the lift, and having a huge laugh at my expense.

19.15, The Hyatt's sports bar

Finished for the day, and time for the obligatory second-day-of-the-shoot drinks. Get thrown out of the bar because Isla looks so young and she doesn't have her passport with her. She's 22, but has the peachy, dewy skin of a teenager . . .

TUESDAY 5 MAY

08.00, Parc St Charles Hotel lobby

Day three of the shoot. Today is a physical and mental challenge: we're shooting two complete stories (the true history of poker, and the roots of rock) so we're all psyched up. I'm so intent on getting together the right props (the Southern Belle dress for Isla, plus some special Scoop playing cards), that I miss the blindingly obvious thing that could go wrong with today, and completely stymie our carefully worked out schedule.

We drive half-an-hour to our first location, the *Boomtown Belle* riverboat gambling palace, which looks authentically turn-of-the-century in the shiny morning light. We get parked, unload the van, meet our contact . . . and get stopped dead by security. 'How old are you, young 'un?' says a short, fat angry looking guy to the beautiful, famous, Isla Fisher. 'Twenty-two,' she tells him. He just laughs, and demands to see her passport – which is in her safe, back at the hotel. It's illegal to let anyone under 21 into a place of gambling in the State of Louisiana, and they're making no exceptions for beautiful young stars . . .

9.45, The *Boomtown Belle*, take 2

Isla and I get back to the boat with her passport, which the short fat guy studies for at least ten minutes before letting us on board, where the director is pacing the floor. Disaster two: in our absence, a strong wind has whipped itself into a frenzy, and we can't take the boat out on the Mississippi after all. We have to re-think our arty first shot, which involved Isla looking gorgeous in her Southern Belle dress doing a PTC on the prow of the *Boomtown Belle* as the boat chugs down the Mississippi. In the end we're forced to do the whole shoot in the dimly lit, flocked-wallpaper-gloom of the boat's inside gambling room. The story still has plenty of strong information about the origins of phrases like 'to give someone the brush off' and 'to pass the buck', but it's not going to look too great . . .

14.30, Louis Armstrong Park, New Orleans

Disaster three: we arrive at the Louis Armstrong Park, where we've arranged to meet the Lil' Rascals brass funk band to film the guts of our music story, only to find that the park is all locked up, and there's no one around. I spent days setting this up – I have faxes galore between me and the Park Manager, proving that I've got every sort of permission that it's possible to get, with insurance liability cover and everything, but I don't think the director wants to see them right now.

I scale the fence, run to an official-looking building, and ask the laid-back security guard about how to get the crew into the park. He doesn't know anything about us filming, and he couldn't be less interested, and the Park Manager has gone on holiday, apparently – but he says we can get in the back way, and he really doesn't care what we do when we get in, nor how long it takes us.

15.30, Louis Armstrong Park

At last, the Lil' Rascals turn up. They were supposed to be here an hour ago, but time seems to be a flexible concept to musicians. The director stopped speaking to me at exactly 15.00.

The band are fabulous. They look fantastic, and play like a dream, and their music lifts our spirits up out of our boots. All eight of them fall instantly in love with Isla, and so resolve to work very hard indeed. Amazingly, we knock off the whole story in less than three hours, including five short music numbers, and a deeply moving interview about how the park was a weekly meeting place for slaves during New Orleans' plantation past. It was here that jazz was born, and the memories echo around the park in the late afternoon sunshine.

19.30, Parc St Charles Hotel

I have two scripts to mark up, Isla has to learn tomorrow's pieces to camera, and the crew and director want to run through tomorrow's rodeo story; the most complicated so far. Everyone is hungry and sunburnt and exhausted. Early night.

WEDNESDAY 6 MAY

08.00, Parc St Charles lobby

Day four of the shoot. We set off for a long drive to the little Louisiana town of Zachary. We're late leaving, which puts the director in a bad mood and means that we have to drive very fast. Matthew and Tim are doing 90 miles an hour when the crew van gets a blow-out. Matthew stops the van safely on the shoulder, and changes the tyre in record-breaking time. We resolve to drive more slowly, even if we lose valuable shooting time (see Chapter 9, Health and Safety). Get to the location at 10.30. It's home to an interesting family: the kids are all rodeo champions, and their dad is the top rodeo coach in Southern Louisiana. They have a fantastic back yard with a rodeo ring, 20 head of steer, eight horses, and a bucking bronco machine. We knew after the recce that this story was going to be magic, but it really comes alive when Isla gets on a horse – she's fearless. Everything's going so well that the family get carried away, and start suggesting some 'good ideas' to the director. Here's Matthew's description of two of these 'good ideas': 'In the first one, I get to stand on top of a rusty barrel, and become a slalom post for a stallion to gallop around. In the second one, a full-sized steer will charge straight towards me, and one of the cowboys will lasso it just seconds before it hits the camera.' So, a dramatic TV dilemma: will Matthew agree to do the shots? Will Patrick let him do the shots? Will the steer stop just in time? Tune in to Chapter 9 for an in-depth look at this story – and find out what Patrick and Matthew decide to do . . .

We work solidly until just after 6 in the searing, sweaty heat, and we don't get home until well after 8, but everyone is full of happiness and mutual congratulations. Matthew is particularly happy, just to be alive.

THURSDAY 7 MAY

06.30, Parc St Charles lobby
Shoot, day five. Early start to drive down to the southern-most part of Louisiana for our white alligator story. Everyone is subdued and very tired. This morning we're doing the first part of a complicated story about the only white alligators in the world (not albinos, but a brand new

branch of the Mississippi Alligator species). We have to explain what these creatures are, how they came to be, where they were found, where they are kept now, how they became Louisiana's unofficial mascot, why they can never be set free into the wild, and how scientists plan to breed some more using their understanding of how recessive genes work. Phew!

09.00, Golden Meadows Alligator Facility

Arrive at the secret breeding location where the white alligators are kept. They are gorgeous – blue-eyed blondes with a skin like white chocolate. We do some impressive wildlife filming, including some scary close-up shots of gators feeding. The guy in charge of the gators thumps some of the really big ones on the nose a few times with a pole, so they snarl at the crew and show their teeth to the camera. Matthew and Tim are impressively brave. We also get some good documentary stuff of Isla helping the scientists to sex some baby gators (if they're girls, it's possible that they will carry the white gene).

We work hard up until lunch, which is kindly prepared for us by the alligator handlers. Isla wonders out loud if they washed their hands first, and we all toy with the suspiciously meaty sandwiches . . .

14.30, New Orleans Superdome

Back in the city again for the second part of the Superdome story. First thing to do is to get Isla changed into the same clothes she was wearing on Monday afternoon. Next thing to do is to scare Matthew some more. He has to do some shots from the roof scaffolding, 200 feet above the new ice rink.

Because of the complicated nature of the structure, Matthew has to stand on a tiny platform, holding the camera at arm's length, absolutely rock solid, for several minutes. The camera weighs about 13 kilos.

Now the bit we've all been waiting for – we get to see the new ice rink finished, with the ice dancers rehearsing on it. Hah! The dancers, of course, don't want to be filmed, even though I set this up weeks ago. We lose half an hour's shooting time, while I negotiate. I keep calm, and explain that we've come half way around the world to film this, and we can't go home without the shots. Finally, we're allowed to shoot some skating. I discover that Matthew has filmed the rehearsals, anyway, while I was negotiating. (For the record, Matt says you can get some fine footage if you just leave the camera on a table, accidentally turned on.) Of course we would never have used the shots if we hadn't been given permission. Honest . . .

During the shooting of the closing PTC, the director and I have a continuity row. We need to do a pick-up for an over-the-shoulder shot of Isla looking at a giant notice board. The director wants to know which way she was looking when we did the master shot on Monday. But a lot has happened since Monday. I think she was looking left to right – I'm nearly sure of it – but I didn't make a note of it, and I don't sound too confident. So we get Monday's tape out, and play it back in the camera to check. (I was right, she was looking left to right, but I can hardly say 'I told you so', as I wasn't even convinced myself.)

In the old days of television – well, as recently as the early 1990s – it was usual to take a PA (production assistant) with you on a shoot like this. She would be in charge of continuity as well as taking the time-code notes and getting coffee and generally looking after everyone. It was brilliant: all the researcher or producer had to do was look after the contributors, keep an eye on the story and the schedule, and anticipate the next set up for the director. But it was an expensive way to go about things. Nowadays, we still use PAs for studio and drama shoots, but they're used less and less on factual or documentary shoots. So people like me have to watch out for continuity as well as being in charge of the stories.

16.00, Still at the Superdome

Just one more thing to do: some pick-up PTCs from Isla in a sports stadium for another story which was shot elsewhere. We had hoped to knock off these bits in the Superdome, but the newly-laid ice needs a huge generator to keep it cool until showtime. It clunks into action just as we're about to roll, and Tim the sound recordist just looks at me, sadly shaking his head. Time for a re-think. The Superdome PR woman kindly offers to take us to a nearby sports ground, where we should be able to film without permits or permission.

17.30, In a New Orleans park

Almost finished! Well, we would be if that train would just go away. Sadly, the sports ground location is right next to a railway. Have you any idea how long American freight trains are? This one goes on forever . . .

FRIDAY 8 MAY

07.30, Parc St Charles lobby

Shoot, day six. Meet to travel way down south again to swampy land. Today we're shooting on an alligator farm – the alligator farm, in fact, where the nest of white babies was found 11 years ago. This is an important part of the white alligator story, but we also want to explain how alligator farming works (well, have you ever seen an alligator ranch?), and how it was farming that saved the Mississippi Alligator from extinction due to over-hunting during the sixties and seventies. But the best bit of today's work will be watching Isla release more than 20 almost fully grown gators into the swamp.

Here's the scoop on gator farming: most baby gators born into the Louisiana bayou get killed before they even hatch out of their eggs: the waters are teeming with predators who just love to snack on gatorlets. So, gator farmers are allowed to collect as many gator eggs as they like during the summer months, which they hatch and raise in special gator pens. Once the babies have grown up into 4-foot-long gators who are big enough and ugly enough to look after themselves, the farmers release 17 percent of them back into the wild again.

So the good news is that we get to go way out on the bayou in a convoy of airboats and speedboats – more fun than any of us have had in years! The bad news is that, for part of the journey, we're in a boat with 20 pissed-off alligators who don't realise we're doing them a favour. And the really bad news for Isla is that she gets to take the tape off their mouths, before they get flung back where they belong!

She is spunky, that girl. My unofficial tip for finding presenters would be: always use an Australian. Soon she's picking up gators, and untying them herself, even though they're covered in alligator muck, which she's getting all over her good white trousers.

I get extra brownie points from the crew because I remembered to bring sunscreen and bug repellent – it's blisteringly hot and we're all getting eaten to death by mosquitoes.

15.00, Back at the alligator ranch

Pick up all the shots and PTCs we need to set up the release sequence. Everyone is de-mob happy now, and we have a silly golf-cart race in between the hard work. Matthew is in such a good mood that he hardly minds a bit when something really, really horrible happens to him. Patrick the director wants some shots inside the baby gator pens. Trouble is, the pens are dark, and as soon as you open the door, the babies disappear off into the corners. So Patrick asks Matthew to start rolling, then open the door and run in, so he can get a few shots before the babies merge into the shadows. Matthew starts to roll, and opens the door . . . and a hundred enormous cockroaches land on his head, and scuttle all over his body.

18.00, Parc St Charles Hotel

We get back to the hotel in time to pack up the thirty tapes we've shot this week and take them to the Fedex office. The tapes and my marked-up scripts are being shipped back to the UK, where our editor will start a rough cut. Meanwhile, the rest of us are only half-way through our filming trip: the director and I are going to New York tomorrow to meet another presenter and another crew, for another week of filming. And Isla and this crew are off to Los Angeles at four in the morning to meet up with the other half of the production team. But we all feel deliriously happy. We got some great stuff this week.

20.00, The bar of the Parc St Charles Hotel

We meet for drinks for the last time, before heading out for a Cajun evening. I feel a bit emotional – it's a funny feeling when you have to say goodbye after a week of intense team work. We play the traditional last-day-of-the-shoot-game, called 'What Was Your Favourite Moment?'. The cameraman says it was the rodeo for him, particularly the bit where the charging steer nearly killed him. The sound guy says, definitely the music item – what a challenge! The director plumps for the wide shot of the Superdome, which he thought was spectacular, and cleverly revealed. For Isla, the magic moment was when she held her first alligator, and then set it free into the swamp. And for me, my favourite bit is right now, this very moment, when it's all over, and the stories worked.

2

Which Job is Best for You?

If you're browsing through this book in a bookshop, you already know that you'd like to work in television, but maybe you're not sure what you'd do. This is something you need to address right away – it's important to know which area you want to aim for, *before* you start applying for jobs (you can always change tack later on). There are lots of good ways to get into TV. If you're artistic; consider jobs like graphic or set design, or makeup and costume. If you're fit, with a good eye for detail you could go for a job in props, or think about training to be an electrician, or a grip. If you're good with your hands, there are craft jobs like painting or carpentry (becoming a joiner may not be the most obvious TV career choice, but somebody needs to build the sets!).

These are all good ways in; they all need specialist skills though, and most of them require a specialist education or training. We'll look at the kind of qualifications you need to do them later in this chapter. But the bulk of this book will concentrate on how to get the most popular television jobs: researcher, camera operator, sound recordist, editor, dubbing mixer, floor/unit manager, PA . . . the jobs that media graduates tend to go for.

Just for fun, here's a short personality quiz to help you decide which TV job would suit you best and make you happiest. By the way, if you are browsing through this book, you might like to go and buy it now. This is not a library. Unless you're browsing through it in a library, in which case it is.

A TV PERSONALITY QUIZ

So, which one of these personality types sounds most like you:

1.   You are naturally and irrepressibly nosy – it's your idea of fun to phone up complete strangers and ask them outrageous questions. Although you are fearless and spunky, you're also caring and sympathetic. You do like to be in control of situations.

2. You can do three very difficult things at the same time, without getting stressed, or losing your concentration, or swearing at anyone. You have the patience of a saint, the strength of an ox, and the reactions of a wild-west gunslinger.

3. You have a passion for new technology that some people might describe as unhealthy. You are quietly confident and never seek approval. You are happy to fit in with other people, and go along with what everyone else is doing.

4. You love to sit alone in a darkened room, fiddling with your equipment. It's your mission in life to fix the terrible mistakes caused by people less talented than you. You have an unusual personality: thick-skinned, yet also sensitive to other people's moods.

5. You have the voice of God, and a calm, collected confidence that is the envy of all your friends. People turn to you in a crisis. You never lose your cool, and never say 'I told you so'.

6. You have nerves of steel, a head for figures, and a heart of gold – which is sometimes disguised by your tendency to be a bit of a bossy-boots.

7. You long to travel, save the rainforests, and meet fabulously glamorous people.

Answers

WHICH JOB IS BEST FOR YOU?

1. You are naturally and irrepressibly nosy – it's your idea of fun to phone up complete strangers and ask them outrageous questions. Although you are fearless and spunky, you're also caring and sympathetic. You do like to be in control of situations.

If you picked 1, you're a natural television researcher. This may surprise you – surely researchers are studious, bookish types who seek out information and impart knowledge? Yes and no. Finding things out *is* an important part of being a researcher, but you'll spend more time on the phone than in the library. One of the most important parts of being a researcher is persuading people to do things – whether it's giving you information, or allowing you to film them. Of course you'll also be expected to come up with brilliant ideas. And you'll learn how to turn your ideas into scripts. Eventually you'll be able to capture magic on tape when you become a director. But your core job will be phoning people up, being charming to them, and getting them to do things for you. (If the very idea of cold-calling strangers terrifies the life out of you, see Chapter 6 for tips on how to schmooze.) All good researchers are deep-down nosy, and eternally curious: if you're the sort of person who is often to be found exclaiming 'How interesting!', 'How does that work?', 'Why should that be?', 'Why does that happen?', then you will love being a researcher. If you're not that bothered about finding things out, you'll hate it. And the control bit? One day you will probably become a producer or director, so you'll have to tell all these other people what to do. Shrinking violets need not apply.

WHICH JOB IS BEST FOR YOU?

2. You can do three very difficult things, all at the same time, without getting stressed, or losing your concentration, or swearing at anyone. You have the patience of a saint, the strength of an ox, and the reactions of a wild-west gunslinger.

Number 2 is a job description for a camera operator. It's a fulfilling and creative job, but you will need huge reserves of diplomacy and understanding to get the most out of this career choice. Because here's the thing – directors rarely have time to say 'please' and 'thank-you'. They will bark instructions at you, expecting you to leap into action at their command, even though you've been hanging around for ages while they made up their mind what to shoot. Then once things get moving, you must follow their every whim exactly and to the letter – except when they've made a mistake, in which case you must anticipate what they really wanted to do, get the shot they missed, and save their bacon. When this happens, you must never mention it, because the director is always right.

Seriously, you need very special skills to be a professional camera operator. This may surprise you; nowadays almost everyone can use a video camera, and most of us know how to shoot stuff – you just point the camera in the right direction, and try not to cut people's heads off. What marks out a professional camera operator is the ability to frame a shot quickly and elegantly, while scores of highly-paid people stand around waiting for him to get it right. And while he's framing the shot, he's probably zooming in with his right hand, pulling focus with his left hand, and rotating his whole body with absolute controlled precision to create a perfect pan. It's ballet and weightlifting combined.

WHICH JOB IS BEST FOR YOU?

3. You have a passion for new technology that some people might describe as unhealthy. You are quietly confident and never seek approval. You are happy to fit in with other people, and go along with what everyone else is doing.

If you picked 3, then I'm afraid you're a sound recordist at heart. For it's a universal truth that sound recordists are nerds. Perhaps it's something to do with being shut off from the world all day, headphones clamped to their skull, twiddling knobs and studying level meters. Certainly, the attention to detail required to be a good sound recordist demands a certain, well, nerdiness, and I mean that in the best possible way. Many of them are extremely talented nerds. Some are well-dressed, attractive nerds. A few are even genius nerds, whose work can turn a good programme into a great one. But they're all nerds. And it's a good thing too – every crew needs a nerd. They're great at fixing equipment, they always have the latest, most high-tech mobile phone, and they know a great deal about obscure subjects, which can sometimes come in handy. And when the shoot's over, they always know the best place to eat.

Sound recordists need to be secure in their own abilities; approval junkies need not apply. Because here's something you never, ever hear a director saying: 'Thank you for the wonderful sound you recorded today.' Just doesn't happen. Sadly, people only notice sound when it goes wrong. And here's another strange thing about sound recordists – on location, they are attached to the camera by a long curly wire. Think about this for a minute, and imagine you're a sound recordist. You have to go wherever the camera goes. If the camera operator is covering a difficult piece of action, you have to anticipate what's going to happen next, and position yourself so that you and your equipment are always out of shot. One wrong move from you and the whole sequence is ruined. Sound recording is a physically and mentally challenging job. Recently I met a media student who was planning to apply for a job in sound because it was 'an easy option'. Well, here's the scoop on that score: in TV, there are no easy options.

WHICH JOB IS BEST FOR YOU?

4. You love to sit alone in a darkened room, fiddling with your equipment. It's your mission in life to fix the terrible mistakes caused by people less talented than you. You have an unusual personality – thick-skinned, yet also sensitive to other people's moods.

If number 4 rings your bell, you could have a happy life in post-production. Editors and dubbing mixers join the production late in the day, when everything has already been shot, and it's too late to get that crucial wide-shot, or record that all-important wildtrack. Editing, like carpentry, is a deeply satisfying job because you get to make something tangible, something that you can see developing bit by bit. You also have the satisfaction of knowing that you could have directed the shoot much better, without all the hard work and hassle of actually having to do it. And believe it, a good editor can make a second-rate director look great. The first time I directed a sequence, I made so many mistakes I should have been locked out of the building. But instead, along came a brilliant editor to the rescue. He tactfully suggested a different way to cut my rushes, and then set about putting together a rather good piece of television – so good, in fact, that sane people complimented me on my work.

Dubbing is a fantastic process too; the last step in the production line that is a television programme. Dubbing mixers are perfectionists, they have an almost fanatical attention to detail, and they speak in a funny techno-babble – in some ways they're super-nerds (well, they're sound people, and they don't get out much!). They take all the various bits of sound on a programme – commentary, atmosphere, music, sound effects and dialogue – and mix them so that everything is at the correct levels and in the right place. This bald description doesn't even come close to describing just how clever dubbing really is. It's a subtle art, and if it's done well, the programme will be involving and absorbing and full of atmosphere. If it's done badly, the programme will feel leaden and somehow alienating.

WHICH JOB IS BEST FOR YOU?

5. You have the voice of God, and a calm, collected confidence that is the envy of all your friends. People turn to you in a crisis. You never lose your cool, and never say 'I told you so'.

If you picked 5 then you really are a very special person, for you have the makings of a great floor manager. Imagine the scene: you are standing on a busy studio floor, surrounded by cameras, runners, researchers, makeup people. In front of you, resplendent in the set, is a very famous presenter, and she is throwing a tantrum, a real ten-carat-gold wobbly. Up in the gallery above you, the director is tense – you are about to go live on air to the network. Through your headphones you can clearly hear the commotion in the gallery – at least three people are talking at once. The PA is counting down

'45 seconds to on-air . . .' With half your brain, you listen carefully to the voices in your ear, and with the other half you calmly but firmly take the situation in hand. In the space of 40 seconds, you persuade the star to get on with her job, then you pick up the count-down to on-air, counting down out loud so that everyone on the floor can hear, while at the same time gently relocating a member of the audience who has accidentally wandered into the wide shot. Finally, you slip into position to cue the band for the opening musical number. You go on air, and everything is perfect. You have saved the day, and everyone loves you. Could you do all that? You could? Then floor managing needs you, no doubt about it. Of course, floor managing is about much more than just soothing starry tempers. The true job description is that you're the voice of the director in the studio. You must listen to what the director wants, then *manage the floor* so that everyone on the studio floor is exactly where the director wants them to be, and preferably before the director wants them to be there – thinking ahead is an important floor managing skill.

On location, the floor manager is called a unit manager, or first assistant director. The job is much the same – to be in complete control of the shoot, so that all the director has to think about is directing – but the problems you may have to troubleshoot are incomparably greater. Imagine dealing with 600 extras, in a freak sleet storm in May, when your star has gone missing and you can't get in touch with his driver. Like I said, this is a job for a very special person . . .

WHICH JOB IS BEST FOR YOU?

6. You have nerves of steel, a head for figures, and a heart of gold –
which is sometimes disguised by your tendency to be a bit of a
bossy-boots.

If number 6 sounds like you, then what are you doing sitting
there – get yourself a secretarial job in TV and then train to
become a PA (production assistant). PAs used to be an
indispensable part of every production, but nowadays,
low budget programmes have dispensed with them, and the
PA's work is split between the production secretary (or production coordinator), and the researcher. Only live shows,
dramas and high budget programmes use PAs now, which is
a shame because having a PA on board makes everyone feel
safe. They are highly competent people whose work spans
the whole production. Before shooting starts, they prepare
scripts and set up the filming. During the shoot they log all
the shots and type up a shot list for the editor. They're also
in charge of continuity and timings. And when the shooting's
done, they produce a complicated form which lists every
artist who took part in the programme, plus every piece of
music or archive film used. On a live programme, PAs
do incredibly complicated sums in their head, so that the
programme finishes on time, and doesn't fall off air in an
ungainly fashion. Everyone knows where they are when
there's a PA around.

WHICH JOB IS BEST FOR YOU?

7. You long to travel, save the rainforests, and meet fabulously glamorous people.

And number 7? Sorry, but you're in the wrong book – you need the next manual in the series: *How To Win Beauty Contests.*

So now you know the terrible truth about TV types, it's worth considering where these jobs lead, and where you see your career heading.

CAREER PROSPECTS

First, a thought to cheer you up. Once you get into television, you can do anything and go anywhere – assuming that you have the necessary talent, stamina and enthusiasm for the job (you do have, don't you?). This is not the civil service, and there are no set career progression rules. Having said that, here's what normally happens.

RESEARCH

Researchers tend to become senior researchers, then associate or assistant producers. Some researchers like the job so much, they keep doing it forever. These people are in great demand, because some of the skills needed to be a good researcher are the kind of skills that improve with age. But eventually, most researchers become producers and location directors. (I stress 'location' director, because studio director is a different job – it's so very technical, and demands such split-second attention to detail, that most ordinary mortals would suffer mental meltdown if they tried it. One of the best studio directors I know has just trained to be an airline pilot. The two jobs require very similar personalities.) The great thing about coming up through the research route is that you're allowed to learn on the job and you can progress at your own pace – your work is not 'mission critical' as people who like to use these sorts of phrases would say. If you've got the bottle and the talent, you can come up with a terrific idea, have a go at setting up the story, and even try your hand at writing a script, within weeks of getting your first job. If it's not right, someone else can make it better. Whereas a trainee sound recordist can't have a go until she's absolutely ready (. . .*what do you mean you forgot to plug it in!*).

Being a researcher is a terrific job in its own right: it's the linchpin of a production and the place where great ideas start. But it's also the place where the buck naturally stops, which is probably why most researchers can't wait to move into a job where they can boss crews around and yell things like 'Whose fault is this!', and 'Get on with your work!'.

Getting your foot on the ladder

Some producers insist that new researchers work as 'runners' for a few weeks or even months, before becoming fully-fledged researchers. Most runners are young, inexperienced and so burning with the desire to work in television that they accept little or no financial reward for their efforts. Unscrupulous TV companies exploit this, and use them as unpaid labour. But a good, well-run production will treat its runners with respect; give them some real work to do, and offer the good ones properly-paid jobs as soon as possible. Becoming a runner is an excellent way to get your foot on the research ladder – but do it for a few months only, then ask for a proper job.

CAMERAS AND SOUND

Camera operators

Most camera operators start as trainees, and train for about two years before they're allowed to operate a studio camera, or work as second camera on a drama shoot (at least that's the official line – but in most companies, if you're good at the job, you'll get to do useful work sooner than that). Once they're trained, they're usually hooked, and most camera operators stay on camera forever – their only ambition is to become better and better at camera operating. Most camera people aspire to become senior camera operators or camera supervisors, and the best of the bunch become senior lighting camera operators, which means they get paid lots of money, and they get to shoot dramas. Seems there's something addictive about operating a camera on a television show – when I was researching this book, one executive producer, who used to be a cameraman, confided:

It's just the best feeling to be the person who captures magic moments on film or tape. I had to get out before I caught the bug, or I'd never have moved on.

The ones who do move on from camera operating tend to become lighting directors, and some of those become movie DOPs (Directors of Photography). And a few camera operators go on to become studio directors. I know three ex-cameramen who are now studio directors, and guess what – the crews love them and respect them, because they speak the same language, and understand the problems.

Sound recordists

Sound people also start as trainees. And they too tend to stay in sound forever, because sound is what they like and understand. It's their idea of heaven to be let loose on a great big studio mixing desk, or perhaps to record sound on a top-notch location drama. Rarely, one breaks out and becomes a studio director, but it's going against the grain. On the whole, a sound recordist's ambition is to be better at sound recording.

POST-PRODUCTION

Editors and dubbing mixers usually start as post-production runners, then become trainees, and after about two years they get to do some proper editing or mixing. Very few people move out of post-production and into other areas, possibly because post production supervisors like to hire people who will stay editors and dubbing mixers for the duration of their careers. It takes a long time and a lot of money to train somebody to be a good editor – you don't want them nipping off to do something else just when they've finally mastered the job. Here's what the Head of

Post Production for one of the major network companies has to say on the subject:

> 'Some media students seem to be under the impression that becoming an editor is a good route to getting a job as a director. They couldn't be more wrong. I'm not interested in hiring someone who wants to be a director – I'm looking for someone whose life's ambition is to be the best editor in the industry.'

For the record, editors don't always make good directors anyway. You'd think they would – after all they sit there day after day, making a director's work look better, muttering things like: 'Where's the wide shot!' and 'Oh my God, she hasn't done any cutaways, I don't believe this!'. But being wise after the event doesn't necessarily mean that you would be able to do the job yourself.

I know a documentary editor called Jon, who was once given the chance to direct, and do you know what? He was, let's just say, a bit disappointing. He didn't have the temperament for the job (directing is 100 percent all the time – you can't let your attention slip for a second), and he just couldn't see the big picture because he spent so much time concentrating on individual shots. He was so depressed by his efforts, he never asked to do any directing again. But don't feel too sorry for him, he's still a brilliant editor.

FLOOR/UNIT MANAGING

So you dream of being a drama director or producer? Then floor or unit managing is the career route for you. Generally, floor managers should also be able to unit manage; someone who works exclusively in the studio isn't cost-effective. At some network companies, floor/unit managers also work as location managers, which means that they find locations, and are then in charge of the location during the shoot. To complicate things further, unit managers are also called first assistant directors. Floor/unit managers/first assistant directors (henceforth to be known as FUMFADs) all start as runners, then work their way up to become third assistant directors – 'thirds' for short. Thirds become 'seconds', and 'seconds' eventually become 'firsts', except in some companies, where the roles of 'thirds' and 'seconds' are combined into a completely new title, like 'unit assistant' or 'organisational floor manager'. Are you following so far?

The work of a FUMFAD
Here's what they all do:

Once a production has started shooting, the 'third' works as the assistant to the 'first' on location – getting extras ready, and organising everyone into the right positions – because the 'first' is tied to the camera (not literally, you understand), awaiting the director's instructions.

The 'second' is the person behind the scenes. Seconds rarely visit the set. They spend their time back at base, carrying out the first's instructions: coordinating transport, planning ahead to make sure all the props and people are in the right places, issuing call sheets, and generally making sure that the whole production runs like a military operation. Seconds also get to do some scheduling, which is a very important part of the FUMFAD's job – scheduling means taking a script, breaking it down into bits, and working out which scenes to shoot on what days. On a big drama, working out the schedule is an enormous task.

The first, as you've probably gathered by now, is a very important person – he's in overall charge of all the logistics for the studio or location shoot, so that all the director has to do is direct. It's such an important job that many FUMFADs keep doing it forever, but some do move on to become drama production managers, or associate producers, as they're sometimes known in the TV drama world (see next section for job description of production manager). And some FUMFADs keep going until they become drama producers or directors.

SECRETARIAL/ADMINISTRATION

If you join a TV company as a secretary, you have three possible career paths.

Becoming a production manager

The most common path is to train to become a production secretary, then a PA, and then – if you're tough enough – a production manager. Production managers are powerful people.

It's their job to track the production's budget, hire staff and facilities, keep a check on schedules and generally manage the whole production so that the producer can concentrate on the creative stuff. A producer with a good production manager is a very happy producer indeed. Sometimes you get überproduction managers who oversee all the productions for a whole department, or – if it's an independent – for the whole company.

Becoming a personal assistant

The second secretarial career choice is to become a personal assistant to a head of department.

Becoming a researcher

The third path is rarer than the first two, but it does happen regularly – some secretaries become researchers. I can think of at least four excellent researchers who started in a secretarial/administration job, and impressed their bosses so much that they were given the chance to research. You can read the story of how one of them did it in Chapter 3.

Like I said, if you're good enough, and you work hard enough, you can do anything in television.

OTHER WAYS IN

Here's a quick look at some of the other jobs I mentioned at the beginning of this chapter, and the skills and qualities you'd need if you wanted to pursue them.

Makeup

Some makeup artists have studied hairdressing and beauty therapy; others have gone to art or film school, and have degrees in something like drama or art and design. And most have worked in theatre doing wigs and makeup, before getting their first television job. You need an artistic disposition, a likeable personality, and a strong mothering instinct – a makeup artist's work is close and intimate, and they have to deal with actors and presenters when they're at their most insecure.

Costume

This is an 'arty' job too – the costume designer has a big influence on the final look of a programme. Among the many skills you'll need for this job are:

◆ a knowledge of period dress

◆ an understanding of television lighting and how it affects the colour of different fabrics

◆ and a feel for characters, and how different personalities would dress.

Wardrobe and costume designers tend to come from the fashion industry, or from an art school background, and many work in theatre before breaking into television.

Set design

This is a highly specialised job. First, you need to be able to draw, then you need a degree in something like art and design, or architecture or stage design, or interior design (or something else design-y – you get the picture.) Again, lots of set designers start in theatre before moving into TV. But you'll also need strong leadership qualities, a good business sense, and a feel for budgets – you'll be in charge of a lot of people and you'll have to be tough with them and bring their work in on budget and on time. You should also have a director's eye. It's a big job.

Graphic design

If you're arty and you have a way with computers, you could have a fabulous life as a graphic designer. It's a wide-ranging job: one day you could be deciding on the lettering for a show's end credits; the next you could be called upon to produce some animation. Obviously you need to be a competent artist, but nowadays you also need to understand computer technology. An art degree or some sort of graphic design degree is a must.

Props

Props people are in charge of putting up the scenery, but they also have to look after all the little fiddly props like vases and other bits of decoration that might be required on a set. They need to be strong, with a good eye for detail, and a light touch. Many of them have a theatre background.

Grips

Grips are in charge of all the equipment on big location shoots: car mounts, cranes, dollies and tracks, as well as cameras. They also lay the tracks for tracking shots, which is an art in itself. They need to have an encyclopedic knowledge of television equipment, and how to rig it. For all these reasons, they too need to be strong. Grips learn on the job.

Sparks

Sparks are television electrical technicians. They're in charge of all the lighting equipment, and they're also responsible for electrical safety. They need to be strong enough to rig heavy lights. They need to be able to work fast and accurately. They also need to be qualified electricians. Some sparks work in theatre before moving into TV.

Crafts

'Crafts' is the catch-all title for the jobs of painters, carpenters (chippies) and drapesmen.

◆ Painters and carpenters often start as apprentices straight from school, but some come fully trained from theatre, and others have learned their trade doing shopfitting work, or exhibition work, before moving into TV.

◆ Drapesmen (for they do tend to be men) are people who are in charge of fabrics. There's a huge amount of fabric used in television – studios are swathed in the stuff.

Craft workers need all the usual television attributes (good at teamwork, good at taking direction, good at working under difficult conditions and not moaning about it, and good at working very quickly) but they also need to be extra flexible because they can be called upon to work unsociable hours – sometimes even working right through the night – to get a set ready in time.

Part 2
Getting Into TV

'New entrants to TV often forget to do their homework. Don't blow your big break.'

Barbara Govan, Chief Executive,
Screenhouse Productions

3

Getting a Job as a Researcher

Getting a job as a researcher deserves a chapter all to itself, because it's different from getting any other television job. Here's the first and most important difference: you can target individual producers. Never underestimate the power of these words: 'I love your programme'.

Say them again: 'I love your programme'.

Do they give you a warm fuzzy glow? They do? That's amazing, because you haven't even made a programme yet. Now imagine you are a hard-working producer, sweating blood and tears to make great television. In your average day, you – as a successful television producer – are faced with many headaches and heartaches: your budget is blown to smithereens, your presenter hates you, and your ratings are rubbish. It's your job to encourage your staff and make them feel good about themselves. But nobody ever says a kind or encouraging word to you. Until one day, a letter lands on your overflowing in-tray. It starts with the magic words: 'I love your programme . . .'. Wouldn't you – as the hardworking, misunderstood producer – like to meet this person?

Of course it's not quite as simple as that – it'll take more than a bit of shameless flattery to secure your dream job – but showing a genuine interest in someone's programme is an excellent way to start. And it makes a refreshing change from most of the letters and e-mails that producers receive, which tend to concentrate exclusively on the many talents of the writer.

WRITING A GOOD LETTER

The point of your letter is to get you in the door. Once you have secured yourself a face-to-face interview, your natural charm and enthusiasm will have a chance to shine. But until then, you're up against stiff opposition, because most producers get several letters a week from educated, bright young things who want to be researchers. So, how to make sure that your letter stands out?

A good letter should be four things:

◆ specific

◆ short

◆ well written

◆ enthusiastic.

Let's look at those in order (see sample letter page 50.)

Point one
By specific, I mean that the letter should be tailored to appeal to the person who's going to receive it. This may

seem blindingly obvious to you, but you should see some of the letters that producers get.

Example: a friend of mine runs a production company that specialises in top-notch science programmes. But she gets scores of can-I-have-a-job letters from arts graduates, whose letters make it clear that they have no interest in science. She, quite naturally, finds this sort of behaviour tiresome: 'They all want jobs as researchers, yet they can't even be bothered to visit our website, or do some basic research to find out what kind of programmes we make.'

Here's my top letter-writing tip: it's better to write three or four well-researched, well-thought-out letters to particular producers, than to send out a blizzard of standard letters to everybody who ever made a television programme. And it should go without saying that you never, ever, ever write a 'Dear Sir/Madam' letter. Always write to *someone,* make sure you spell their name correctly, and give them their proper title.

Point two

Next point: short is always good. Don't waffle. And please resist the temptation to talk yourself up (I know *you* wouldn't do anything like that, but it's worth saying anyway). Producers have heard it all before – whatever it is.

Catherine Dean
34 Hollyhocks Street
Canterbury, Kent CT2 1GH

Tel: 01227 XXXXXX
Mobile: 0775 XXXXXX
Parents' House: 01225 XXXXXX

30th October, 200X

Paul Carlton
Producer 'Mad Science'
Big Picture Productions
The Old Stables
234 Crescent Road, Leeds LSI 4BT

Dear Paul Carlton

I'm a 22-year-old chemistry graduate, looking for my first proper television job. I've already done some work experience with a production company in Bristol.

I am a big fan of your show 'Mad Science', and I wondered if you had any vacancies for a junior researcher/runner on the next series? I phoned your office, and your assistant told me that production starts in January.

I have lots of ideas for items – for instance, have you thought about thixotropic liquids? Custard would make a great demo: when you stir it quickly, it becomes so thick that you can't move the spoon, but when you stir it gently, the spoon glides through the liquid. So, if you had enough custard, you should be able to run on it – the custard should solidify at the point where your feet hit the surface (as long as you move fast enough, and with enough force). I thought it would make a great item to see the presenter run across a huge bath of custard!

If you would like to meet me, I'd be happy to come to Leeds. I'm working in a music shop at the moment, but I'm always free on Fridays.

I look forward to hearing from you.
Yours sincerely,

Catherine Dean

Fig. 1. A sample letter.

Point three

Your letter must be well-written. If you do get a job as a researcher, you will be expected to be able to write: letters to contributors, briefing notes, treatments, billings, and even scripts. A clumsy, badly punctuated letter is not a good advertisement for your writing skills.

Point four

And finally, be enthusiastic. Science producers are looking for people who are passionate about popular science. Documentary producers want people who are passionate about documentaries. Children's producers want researchers who are passionate about children's programmes. Communicate your passion!

All these things are true for e-mails too.

BUILDING A GOOD CV

What qualifications do you need?

Whatever kind of programmes you want to make, it's good to have an academic degree. Any degree – zoology, French, physics or history – would be just fine. But you should know that not all producers are keen on graduates with media degrees.

Before I explain why, time for a quick digression: do you know the difference between media and media studies?

◆ 'Media studies' is an academic degree, where you analyse media in all its forms (if you're interested in where

Channel 4 gets its funding, or you're keen to examine the symbolism of the pub in *Eastenders,* then media studies is for you).

◆ 'Media', on the other hand, is a completely different sort of degree, which should teach you professional skills like how to edit television programmes, or how to write for magazines. So media studies is supposed to be a theoretical course, while media is supposed to be a practical one.

So is a degree in media a good thing? Yes, maybe and sometimes. If you're going for a job as a camera operator, it's good to have a degree in media, because you'll know one end of the camera from the other. But getting a job as a researcher is different. Producers are looking for bright people with lively, inquiring minds, who will eventually make their own programmes. And making programmes is not about television, it's about reflecting the world. Some of the producers I spoke to when I was researching this book seemed slightly suspicious of graduates who had chosen to do their degree in media or media studies, for three reasons:

◆ A degree in zoology, or French, or physics shows an interest in the world, whereas a degree in media shows only an interest in television.

◆ A media degree is perceived to be easier than a physics or French degree, so it can look as though media students are opting for a lazy way to get a university education.

◆ Media degrees got a bad reputation during the 1990s, when the academic world went mad for media courses.

Some universities and colleges were so keen to jump on the bandwagon that they ended up offering poor-quality courses, that produced poor-quality graduates.

The good news is that things are changing. There are some excellent courses on offer now (see Chapter 5 for information on how to find them), and there are plenty of well-respected people working in television today who came from a media background; their influence is bound to have an effect on the bias against media degrees. And it has to be said that there are two big advantages to doing a media degree: the good courses will help you organise your work experience at a television company; and you'll get useful experience in operating cameras and editing equipment (see Technical Knowledge, later in this chapter).

But all producers like researchers with a broad, well-rounded education. So if your main degree is in media, you may have to work extra hard on the rest of your CV to make sure that your interests don't appear to be limited to television. (See sample CV page 57.)

SPECIALIST SKILLS

Journalism

Journalism is a great way into TV. There are more news programmes than ever before – it's one of the few thriving areas in the industry. You can make a life out of television journalism, or you can use it as a stepping stone towards working in other areas. I started my TV career as a regional journalist, and it's interesting to reflect on what's happened to the people who worked alongside me at the time:

♦ B runs a successful independent production company

♦ P is a hot-shot international executive producer

♦ R is the managing director of a network television company

♦ M is head of regional programmes at a network television company

♦ H runs a thriving documentary department (at, yes, you've guessed it, a network television company)

♦ T is a producer at ITN.

Which perfectly illustrates my point: journalism is a fantastic way in to TV, and great training for whatever you want to do when you get there. Working as a journalist will teach you four important skills:

♦ How to spot a good story

♦ How to write for television

♦ How to think quickly

♦ How to shoot and edit your own stories.

The last point is a new development. Once upon a time, not too long ago, all TV journalists covered their stories with the help of a camera crew, then came back and put the piece together with a video tape editor. But that was before the advent of the VJ, or video journalist. This new breed of television news-gatherer is trained to do the whole thing all by herself. She writes the script, she operates the camera and then she edits and dubs her piece ready for transmission. As with all changes in the TV world, some people think this is the best thing that ever happened, while others think it's the worst. Whatever, VJs are here to stay. Of course, television newsrooms won't be entirely staffed by them – some stories are too big, too complicated, or simply too important to be covered by just one person. For the items that require a bit more finesse, there will always be a need for reporter-presenters, specialist news camera operators, and picture-editors.

How do you get a job as a television journalist?

Right now is a great time to get into television journalism. ITV has a new, year-long traineeship scheme, covering basic and advanced skills in voice and presentation; reporting; compliance and law; bulletin-writing; and editing. Every trainee has a 'home' region, but they'll all get the chance to work in another area for a few weeks, so they learn how to handle different ways of doing things – every newsroom has its own house-style and personality. And all trainees will get the chance to work at ITN for two weeks. To apply for this scheme, you'll need either: a qualification from an NCTJ course (National Council for the Training of Journalists); or a degree in Broadcast Journalism from the BJTC (British Council for the Training of Journalists); or some 'equivalent experience' – this covers a wide range of things, from website-writing, through doing a stint in local radio, to running a community newspaper or magazine. But most importantly, you need to have a passion for telling stories.

Two more things to say about the ITV scheme: the first is that it's hoping to recruit trainees from culturally and socially diverse backgrounds. And second, you're not guaranteed a job at the end of the course. But you will have had 12 months of top-notch training, and the chance to make excellent contacts in TV newsrooms across the company, so it's safe to say that the good people will get good jobs. You can find out more about the ITV journalism training scheme on the company's website: www.itvjobs.com. ITV also runs a bursary scheme, sponsoring several students every year through a BJTC-accredited course.

The BBC runs a broadcast journalist trainee scheme too, offering on-and-off-the-job training in news and current affairs. Details on the BBC's website, or you could send your e-mail address to bbctrainees@bbc.co.uk, to sign up for the quarterly BBC trainees' newsletter.

If you are interested in journalism, a vocational course is useful, because you need to know specific things to be a journalist, such as how to avoid contempt of court, and how the libel laws work. There are hundreds of journalism courses available: print journalism or broadcast journalism; degree courses or post-graduate ones. But here's some advice from another ex-colleague who's now in charge of regional news programmes for a large broadcaster: The best way in to TV news for most people is to do an NCTJ or BJTC course, then get a job in local radio, before applying for a newsroom job at your local ITV or BBC TV station. If you're serious about becoming a journalist, you'll need a good grounding in law and local government. And it helps to have a strong knowledge of local issues.

CATHERINE DEAN

Contact Details

34 Hollyhocks Street
Canterbury Kent CT2 1GH

Tel: 01227 XXXXXX
Mobile: 0775 XXXXXXX
Parents' House: 01225 XXXXXX

D.O.B: 17.7.XXXX

Work History

July 20XX – Present Shop assistant and blues music expert, SmoothSounds, Canterbury. Serving customers, and giving advice on blues and jazz music.

June 20XX – August 20XX Work experience (runner), Avonmouth Films, Bristol. Working on a natural history series, commissioned by the BBC. My main job was to help find archive material, but I did write some briefings and scripts – and I got involved in choosing some of the music.

July 20XX – September 20XX Camp counsellor, Big Lake Summer Camp, San Pedro, California.
Organising edutainment programmes for 10-15 year-olds; looking after the children's welfare; and dealing with the children's homesickness. My big claim to fame is that I taught eight of the campers to juggle!

May 20XX – October 20XX Oxfam volunteer, The Oxfam Shop, Canterbury. Saturday and summer holiday job.

Fig. 2.   A sample CV.

Education

Bath University B.Sc. Chemistry (2.2)

St. Henry's Grammar School, Canterbury 3 A levels: Chemistry (A), Biology (B), Drama (A). 9 GCSEs: Science Double Award (A,B), Maths (A), Drama (A), English (B), French (C), Art (B), History (B), Media Studies (B).

Other Interests

At university, I was part of a drama group – I did some acting, but I was mainly involved in the sound and lighting. The highlight was when I was in sole charge of lighting for seven performances of South Pacific. I also wrote regularly for the university newspaper.

At school, I was chairman of the debating society, and I did backstage work for the drama group. I was also elected year representative on the school council three times.

My hobbies are: jazz dance, playing blues guitar, reading American fiction, hiking and canoeing.

I have a full driving licence.

Referees

Carolyn Blythe,
Executive Producer,
Avonmouth Films,
Bridge Street,
Bristol BS3 1AW
Tel: 0117 XXXXXXX
Mobile: 0787 XXXXXXX

James Shand,
Manager, SmoothSounds,
Station Way,
Canterbury CT1 8TB
Tel: 01227 XXXXX

Fig. 2. *continued.*

Details of NCTJ courses on www.nctj.com/courses. The BJTC has a list of its courses on www.bjtc.org.uk – you can contact them for details of ITV's bursary scheme.

Other skills

Almost any hobby or interest can be an exploitable skill:

◆ Perhaps you're passionate about politics, and you helped out in a campaign office at the last election. Use your knowledge, and your contacts, to get yourself a job on a political programme.

◆ If you're a French graduate, contact producers of education programmes to see if they can use your language skills.

◆ If you're a sports nut, try for a job as runner or junior researcher on a sport programme.

You may be surprised at your marketable skills. I know a producer who got into TV on the strength of his Nintendo expertise – his first television job was as a researcher on a video games show.

Technical knowledge

When I got my first job, the idea of a researcher operating a camera would have been as shocking as, well, a completely untrained person doing something she had no talent for. But things have changed, and nowadays there are lots of reasons why researchers may be asked to use a camera: undercover filming; low budgets; the interviewee can only do the interview *today* and you don't have a proper crew; the director wants to see what a location looks like and she can't come to the recce; and lots more things that will happen to you that I can only dream of. But you won't be expected to do anything complicated, and the equipment will be easy to use. It's also possible that you may get to do some editing, but again, all you'll be expected to do is to stitch some shots together, and stitching shots together is not really editing.

If you can operate a domestic camcorder, you'll be okay with the camera side of things (by the way, you may be surprised to learn that the hardest thing about self-operating is getting good sound!). And if you can operate a word processor, you'll quickly pick up how to edit a basic sequence. Look at it this way: it's not learning to use the equipment that makes camera operating or editing so hard to master. Just as being able to use a word processor doesn't automatically make you a writer, and passing your driving test doesn't make you a grand prix winner, being able to hack some shots together or shoot a talking-head interview is hardly editing or camera operating in the true sense.

Other things that make you special

Your CV is not just about academic qualifications and specialist skills. It should also reflect the fact that you are a bright, interesting person with a lively, inquiring mind – just the sort of person, in fact, that every television producer is looking for. On your behalf, I asked some top producers what would impress them, and they were pretty much unanimous: they're always impressed by someone who displays:

◆ enthusiasm

◆ an intrepid spirit

◆ and a willingness to learn.

You can make your CV shine by doing something unusual that you are genuinely passionate about, like spending your gap year in Africa, helping volunteers with a baby vaccination programme. Or working at an American summer camp. You don't even need to leave the country – take up the saxophone, or learn white-water canoeing, and you will instantly sparkle in a sea of lacklustre candidates who don't seem to have any interests at all (other than TV).

WRITING YOUR CV

All the usual CV rules apply: keep the information clear, uncluttered and short – don't waffle. Say whether or not you have a full driving licence. And don't leave any suspicious holes in the information.

'I'm always wary of a CV that doesn't have any dates,' said one producer. 'It makes me think that the writer is trying to hide something.'

One more absolutely vital tip: make sure your CV has a phone number where you can be contacted in six months' time, even if it's your parents' number. And if you change your mobile phone, call all the producers who've got your CV, and let them know the new number. Think how awful it would be if you missed out on your big TV break because they couldn't find you . . .

GETTING WORK EXPERIENCE

Now you've got your excellent letter and CV, it's time to get yourself some work experience. Work experience used to be an optional extra, but nowadays it's essential. And because work experience has become a prerequisite to a TV job, getting a placement has become a serious business – expect to be interviewed, just as if you were going for a real, fully-paid job. (By the way, if you're under 18, your chances of getting work experience are slim.)

If you're not on a media course, you need to organise your own placement. Here's how:

◆ Decide which company you'd most like to work for, taking two things into account: first, you're not going to get paid during work experience, so somewhere close to your parents' home or near where you're studying would be best. And second: check that the company makes programmes that interest you. There's no point in applying to a science producer if your passion is for the arts. Working in regional programmes gives you the chance to handle lots of different types of stories – the BBC makes the biggest range of regional programmes.

◆ Meanwhile, put your name down for work experience with the big broadcasters. Details of ITV placements are at www.itvjobs.com. You should also be able to set up a 'jobs account' at this website, which means that you'll get an e-mail when an opening comes up for a placement or a paid job in your area of interest. ITV can offer around 1,000 placements a year across the company, but don't expect more than a couple of weeks' work experience.

If you live in Scotland, you can find out about placements by visiting www.scottishtv.co.uk. BBC work experience places are advertised on the BBC's website: www.bbc.co.uk.

◆ But don't sit around waiting for someone in Human Resources to get back to you – get in touch directly with producers whose work you admire. (Don't forget that researchers can get valuable experience, and make excellent contacts, working at an independent production company.) Send your CV and an enthusiastic letter to the producer you would most like to work for, explaining why you love her programmes, and asking if you could have a five minute meeting with her to talk about getting some work experience.

Next comes the tricky bit – this is where your training to be a researcher really starts – you have to get yourself in the door. My advice would be to follow your letter with a phone call, make friends with the producer's assistant, and ask if you can talk to the producer on the phone. If it's a bad time, find out a good time to call back. You must be determined, but sensitive – don't become a pain in the neck by phoning up every day, but on the other hand, you really need to get yourself a face-to-face interview. It could be that the producer refers your letter to her executive producer. If so, make friends with his assistant too. While you're making friends, you should ask for a couple of tapes of the producer's programmes, and perhaps some of the other programmes that come out of the department.

HOW TO SHINE AT YOUR INTERVIEW

It worked! You're waiting outside the producer's (or executive producer's) office for your informal chat. It doesn't feel informal – you've never been so nervous in your life! Take some deep breaths, wipe your sweaty palms and concentrate on these five useful tips for getting through your first interview:

1. Have some interesting things to say about the producer's programmes, or if you're seeing an executive producer or head of department, have an opinion on the output of the department (this is where those tapes come in handy – the ones that your new friends sent you). Be honest, but also positive. Think of constructive criticisms. Frankly, being a Smart Alec won't do you any good at all. The fact that you've watched the programmes will win you instant brownie points. The fact that you've thought about them, and have interesting things to say, will make you even more popular.

2. Sparkle. The minute you walk through the door, make eye contact and smile. Make sure your handshake is strong and firm. Sit forward on your seat, don't lean back. Remember, producers are looking for enthusiasm. Here's what one head of department said about some of the people who come through his door wanting work experience: 'They're so laid-back they're almost horizontal. I feel as though I want to poke them with a cattle-prod! I'm looking for zip and zest and passion – I can't be doing with wallflowers. I want people with personality in my department.'

3. Have some interesting programme ideas, and share them. There are people who believe that you shouldn't tell anyone your ideas before you've got a job because some producer will pinch them, use them himself, and you'll be left jobless and idea-less. This is nonsense. It just doesn't happen, and here's why – if your ideas are really that good (good enough to rip off) the producer will want to hire you. It's possible that the producer may already be developing an idea that's similar to one of yours, in which case he's going to be even more impressed by you, because your mind is working along the same lines. You can't lose by sharing your ideas.

4. Read Chapter 6 for tips on how to be a good researcher *before* you go for your interview. Your understanding of the job will be impressive.

5. Listen, ask questions, and interact with the producer. Working in TV is all about interacting, having con- versations, and bouncing ideas off other people. Producers are looking for evidence that you're easy to get on with – a large part of your time will be spent on the phone, interviewing people and trying to persuade them to help you. Don't worry about looking nervous (in the words of one seasoned executive producer: 'All the good people are nervous – it shows that they care!'), but don't let yourself get so paralysed with fear that you can't have an interesting conversation.

Finally, some quotes from producers, executive producers and heads of department on what they're looking for in a would-be researcher:

'Someone who's forever curious, and interested in the world around them.'

'Someone who has an interesting way of talking about the mundane.'

'Someone who is serious about making good programmes, but always fun to be with.'

'A team player with bags of character and personality.'

DOING WORK EXPERIENCE

You're not going to believe this, but some people don't make the most of their work experience. In fact there are people who, having landed a fantastic placement, sit there reading the paper all day. Work experience is:

◆ your chance to shine

◆ your chance to share your ideas

◆ and your chance to take on as much real work as you possibly can.

So, ask questions, make yourself useful and offer to do anything that will help the other researchers and producers. And whatever you do, do it with enthusiasm, and to the best of your ability. Turn up early and stay until everyone else has gone home. Look keen. And when your work experience is over, send a handwritten thank-you note. If you do all this, you will be remembered as a fun, enthusiastic, hard-working, interesting and nice person. And next time there's a vacancy for a junior researcher or runner, on a short-term contract, your name will be on everyone's lips.

Andrew is a broadcast journalism graduate who has landed a plum research contract on a BBC documentary series – and all because he made his mark during his work experience.

He won a three-week placement on the series when he was still studying. Many students were interviewed for just one place, but amazingly, Andrew was the only one who'd bothered to watch the programme, and he had 'a lot to say about it'. He made himself useful during his work experience by coming up with ideas on how to film a story about big cats running wild in Lincolnshire.

Andrew's ideas, enthusiasm, and capacity for hard work made such an impression that he was asked to come in to help out on the programme one day a week during his final year at university. 'I learned more on that one day a week than I did during the rest of the year,' says Andrew. Now he's been offered a six month contract with the documentary-making team. It's not glamorous – he's just finished a three-day-and-night stakeout at a landfill site – but it's exciting. 'And there's a real satisfaction in seeing your ideas take shape,' he says.

And remember: Andrew got the job because he was the *only* candidate who'd watched the programme.

TRAINING SCHEMES

The BBC's scheme

Most researchers learn on the job. But every year, a few lucky ones get the chance to start their TV careers on entry-level training schemes. Currently, the best of these are run by the BBC, and the corporation's flagship scheme is called the Production Trainee Scheme. It lasts for 18 months, during which time you get the chance to work in radio, television and new media, doing editing, research, script writing, web production, and working on live studio programmes. You have to sort out your own position at the end of 18 months, but most trainees walk into a production job. Sounds wonderful? It is. But there are thousands of applications for a handful of places. The good news is that this famously 'Oxbridge-only' scheme is trying to attract trainees from culturally and socially diverse backgrounds. The Production Trainee Scheme is advertised in the spring. More information on the BBC's website, or e-mail bbctrainees@bbc.co.uk to sign up for the quarterly BBC trainees' newsletter.

The ITV scheme

Until recently, training in ITV was an *ad hoc* affair – companies recruited fresh faces when they got a few programme commissions. But all that is changing with ITV's new, joined-up approach to training. The new-look ITV is developing entry-level training schemes for researchers, camera operators and sound recordists.

Places on these schemes are limited, and according to one trainer, they'll go to applicants who can 'demonstrate their passion'. She went on to explain: 'We expect to see CVs that reflect a wide range of non-broadcast experience: working in hospital radio and on regional radio programmes; writing for university newspapers; lobbying for community groups and other things that show a commitment to the business of communicating.' All these new training schemes have one thing in common: they're looking to recruit a wide range of trainees from different ethnic and social backgrounds. As one trainer put it: 'We need to widen our pool, which has been traditionally white-middle-class. But that doesn't reflect the audience any more, so we're looking for trainees with different stories to tell, and different points of view to contribute to the company's future.' Details of training schemes on ITV's website: www.itvjobs.com.

OTHER WAYS TO GET YOUR FIRST RESEARCH JOB

There is another way to get your dream job, but it's not for the faint-hearted: take any job you can get in a television company, and work towards your goal. Here's a story about someone who did just that.

Alice had a degree in music, so she applied for a job in the music department of one of the big network companies. She didn't get it (it went to an internal applicant); but she impressed the personnel people, so they suggested her for other positions within the company. She got a job as a secretary, and she impressed her boss so much that she recommended her for a job as production coordinator in the documentary department. In less than a year, she had impressed her *new* boss so much that she was working as a researcher. That was just two years ago. Now she's a senior researcher; about to train as a director. In her own words, here's how she did it:

'I made it clear right from the start that I wanted to research one day, but that I'd do my secretarial jobs whole-heartedly until that day came. When I was a secretary, I'd help out on productions at weekends, or after work. When I was a production coordinator, I went out on shoots in my spare time – at weekends and holidays. By the time I got the research job, I knew how to do it.'

And she added this tip:

'If you're going to get into television this way, you need to be very sure of yourself, and good at whatever you do.'

One final thought about becoming a researcher – it's not like getting a regular job. Most researchers work on short-term contracts, on a programme-only basis. Once they've proved themselves, they get longer contracts which can last for six months to a year. But very few researchers working in television today have staff jobs, and in the future there will almost certainly be no staff jobs at all. Use this to your advantage by getting as much experience as you can, on different types of programmes. And don't worry about where your next job is coming from.

TELEVISION SECRET

Here's a television Secret: if you're good, and enthusiastic, your reputation will spread, and you will get work. There really aren't enough good people to go round.

(4)

Getting Any Other Job

It may seem unfair that getting a research job gets a section all to itself, whereas getting a job as a camera operator has to share a chapter with sound recordists, floor managers, editors, PAs and dubbing mixers. I mean no disrespect to these distinguished careers, it's just that there are lots of common factors to getting these positions. We'll deal with the similar bits first, then look at specific tips for the job that interests you.

First, a warning – you really should know which job you're aiming for, before we go any further. If you still don't know what you want to do, go back and read Chapter 2 again, and keep reading until you feel inspired. I don't want to be boring about this, but TV bosses really dislike letters that start: 'I want to work in television, and I'll do anything . . .' They're not looking for jack-of-all-trades. They want young, passionate people who are burning with the desire to edit, *or* operate camera, *or* floor manage, but not all three. One powerful head of department who hires everybody from camera operators, through floor managers to carpenters, told me:

'I'll-do-anything-letters show a distinct lack of commitment on the part of the writer – why do they want to work in television if they don't know what they want to do? As well as being irritating, these letters are also insulting. We're a network television company, for goodness sake, not some hick operation where jobs are interchangeable.'

You have been warned . . .

THE THREE WAYS TO GET INTO TV

Once you've decided what you really want to do – and it's not research – there are three ways to get into TV.

1. Get yourself a job – any job – in a television company. Insiders have a huge advantage; lots of TV jobs and trainee places are only advertised internally. One way to get a foot in the door is to take a job in the post room. Traditionally in TV, the people who deliver the mail are waiting for a chance to become a runner, with a view to training as a floor manager or an editor.

   'It's an excellent way to make contacts within the building, and you may get the chance to "shadow" in different departments,' said the head of training at one of the big network companies, adding: 'Normally, post-room people move on within 14 to 18 months.'

   If you don't fancy delivering the mail, you could try an administration or secretarial job – this is a good way in if your aim is to become a PA. Also, some television companies recruit department runners, as distinct from runners for particular shows. So if you're passionate about working in drama, you may be able to get yourself a job as a drama department runner. Doing work experience will also get you in the building – we'll look at how to organise work experience in a moment.

2. Get on a specialised trainee scheme. Both ITV and the BBC have recently confirmed their 'commitment' to entry-level training schemes. Which is a jolly good thing as they're the only companies producing a broad enough range of programmes to offer fully-rounded training for jobs such as camera operator, sound engineering, production assistant and floor or unit managing.

Since ITV started to become one big company instead of lots of smaller ones, it's been developing a raft of entry-level training schemes for various craft and crew jobs, including camera operators and sound recordists. Places on these schemes are limited, and according to one trainer, they'll go to applicants who can 'demonstrate their passion'. She added: 'We expect to see CVs that reflect a wide range of non-broadcast experience: working in hospital radio; writing for university newspapers; lobbying for community groups and other things that show a commitment to the business of communicating.' These training schemes are not specifically billed as graduate schemes, but most people who get places on them will have a university degree. However, ITV is also setting up an apprenticeship scheme for electricians and craft jobs.

The BBC operates entry-level trainee schemes for floor managers, sound recordists, camera operators and editors. Traditionally, most of these trainee places have been in London. But the corporation's plans to move some programme-making departments up to Manchester will mean more traineeships in the north.

Both the BBC and ITV are looking to recruit a wide range of trainees from different ethnic and social backgrounds. To check out the latest news on training schemes and apprenticeships, set up a 'jobs account' at www.itvjobs.com, and e-mail: bbctrainees@bbc.co.uk to subscribe to the BBC trainees' newsletter.

3. Get on a 'technical operator' scheme. This is an old BBC idea, currently enjoying a revival at some of the ITV network companies as part of their satellite channel and regional programme output. The idea is that you take on a bunch of enthusiastic young people who want to work in television, and put them to work in rotation, doing different studio-based jobs, so they get a feel for all the jobs, before specialising in one. At the BBC, tech ops only do technical jobs, but in ITV they also floor manage – in fact, some companies have run satellite channels staffed almost entirely with trainee technical operators. It's an idea that some people love, and others hate. Advocates of the tech op schemes say they're a great way for young people to get a feel for all the TV jobs on offer, and decide which one they're best at, with the added bonus that the tech ops actually get to do some proper television work right away (unlike trainees who tend to

train for months, or even years, before they get their hands on a camera or a microphone). Critics of these schemes say they're just a cynical way to get cheap labour, and that anybody worth having should know what they want to do, anyway! Two things are for sure: good people on technical operator schemes do get the chance to learn fast, prove their worth, get noticed, and move on to specialise in the job of their dreams; and tech op schemes are here to stay – they're the only way to budget low-cost, studio-based programmes. (Here's an important thing to say at this point: 'I'll-do-anything-letters' don't go down well with recruiters of technical operator schemes, either. The way to play it is to say that you're interested in sound recording, camera operating, or whatever, but that you would like a broad training before you decide which discipline you want to specialise in.)

Whichever way you choose to make your grand entrance into the television industry, there's one thing you just have to do first: get yourself some work experience. Work experience used to be an optional extra – perhaps something to wile away those long student holidays – but nowadays it's a crucial step towards getting a job in TV. Requests for placements hugely outnumber the places available, so you need to treat your application for work experience as seriously as you would treat an application for a proper, full-time, paid-up job.

GETTING WORK EXPERIENCE

If you're going for a camera, sound or editing job, a media degree is a good thing to have, as long as you're aware that the currency of media degrees has been devalued over the past few years. Everyone has one these days, so you need to do something extra to prove your passion and commitment – like make a film or put together a portfolio of photographs. The great thing about media courses is that the good colleges and universities will help you organise your placement (see Chapter 5 for information on how to pick an industry-approved media course).

If you're not planning to do a media course, here's how to go about organising your own work experience. (By the way, a few of these tips overlap with the advice on how to get a research placement in Chapter 3).

◆ First, decide which company you want to work for. You won't get paid during your work experience, so probably somewhere close to your parents' home or near where you're studying would be best.

◆ In the meantime, put your name down for work experience with the big broadcasters. ITV's website www.itvjobs.co.uk has details of placements. You should be able to apply for one, and also set up a 'jobs account' on this site – which means you'll get an e-mail when an opening comes up for work experience or a paid job in your area of interest. ITV offers around 1,000 placements a year across the company's regional centres, but don't expect more than a couple of weeks' work experience. If you live in Scotland, you can find out about placements by visiting www.scottishtv.co.uk. BBC work experience places are advertised on the BBC's website: www.bbc.co.uk.

◆ But don't sit around waiting for a website to get back to you – go out and find yourself a mentor. Track down someone whose work you admire, and ask them about getting work experience. Whether you want to be a vision mixer or a unit manager, watch the credits, note down names and then get in touch with some real, live people. They'll be flattered by your interest, and they'll be able to give you inside information about opportunities for placements.

◆ Prepare your CV or application form. The two most important things to do at this stage are: highlight your particular interest; and show what you've done to further that interest. For instance, if you're a would-be camera operator, talk about your enthusiasm for photography. In the words of one BBC trainer: 'We need to see evidence that the applicant has gone beyond just doing a media course. We're looking for passion and drive, and a real commitment to the job they're being interviewed for.'

◆ Some more useful tips on preparing your application form: keep it simple and straightforward, don't waffle. Write neatly; TV bosses get hundreds of these forms, so they're looking for an excuse to put as many as possible in the bin – don't lose your chance because your form was illegible. And please don't talk yourself up – be honest, they've heard it all before. Whatever you do, don't send an accompanying CV printed on lime green paper to make yourself stand out. You will stand out all right, but not in a good way. It's fine to have a wacky CV or website once you've established yourself, and won the respect of your peers – but when you're just out of college and you have no reputation, it makes you look a bit, well, dorky.

◆ Send your application to the appropriate person. Make sure you spell their name correctly, and check their correct title. Never write a 'Dear Sir/Madam' letter – they go to the bottom of the pile, along with the 'I'll-do-anything-letters'.

◆ Send off your application in plenty of time – if you're looking for a summer work experience placement, start organising it the previous October.

◆ It's fine to phone up every now and then (but don't become a pain in the neck!) to check how your request for a placement is progressing. But never, ever, ever allow your mum or gran to phone up on your behalf. I know *you* wouldn't do this, but it's worth saying, because personnel people complain bitterly about the astonishing number of bolshie grannies they have to deal with every year when work experience time comes around. If a member of your family does phone up on your behalf it causes bad feeling, and your request could find its way to the bottom of the pile, next to the 'Dear Sir' and 'I'll-do-anything-letters'. If your granny is a meddler, tell her to back off!

◆ If your request for a work experience placement at the TV station of your choice is turned down because all the slots have been taken, ask if you can come in and 'shadow' for a few days. With your charm and personality, a few days might be just enough to make an impression . . .

If the idea of phoning up a television company and actually *talking* to someone fills you with dread, then take heart because you're in good company – everybody thinks that's a scary idea.

Peter is a confident and well-respected drama unit manager, who looks like he takes everything in his stride. But here's what he had to say about getting his first job: 'I just wish I'd taken the time, and had the courage, to phone up companies and ask the simple question: *'Who do I need to write to?'*, before I sent off my CV and hundreds of letters. Most people who answer the phone will be more than happy to tell you who to write to, and give you any other advice you ask for. I think I just had the 'fear factor' – fear not only of being rejected, but also, what if the hirer-and-firer answered the phone and I found myself in the spotlight! So I wasted months of my life sending out letters to 'Dear Sir/Madam', and of course I didn't get anywhere. With hindsight, I now know that it's important to be up front and confident. And even if the worst happens – say someone's having a bad day and they tell you to get lost – well so what, there are lots of other outlets to try. And you could phone the same company a week later and get a totally different response.'

MAKING THE MOST OF YOUR WORK EXPERIENCE

I said this in the last chapter, but you probably didn't read that bit, so I'll say it again: some people don't make the most of their work experience. Amazing isn't it? Believe it or not, there are people who – having landed a fantastic, to-die-for placement – sit around drinking coffee and skiving off on fag breaks. Work experience is your chance to shine; your chance to show just how capable you are. So, ask questions, make yourself useful and offer to do anything that will help the rest of the team you're working with. And whatever you do, do it with enthusiasm, and to the best of your ability – even if you're asked to clean the studio, file some tapes, or make the tea. Turn up early and stay until everyone else has gone home. Look keen. And when your work experience is over, send a hand-written thank-you note to the head of department. If you do all this, you will be remembered as a fun, enthusiastic, hard-working, interesting and nice person. And next time there's a vacancy for a trainee-whatever-you-want-to-be, your name will be on everyone's lips.

QUALITIES AND QUALIFICATIONS

Expect to be interviewed, even if you're going for a work experience placement. Here's a detailed, job by job breakdown of what TV bosses are looking for when they interview you.

CAMERAS

A degree in photography, film and television, or a media degree from a respected university, will look good on your CV (you'll need at least 3 Cs at A-level to get onto a good media course – see Chapter 5). When you turn up for your first TV interview – either for work experience, or for a trainee post – you must be able to display a good knowledge of lighting, optics and electronics; you'll be asked questions like: 'What is meant by "depth of field"?'. But it's your personal qualities that will set you apart from the hundreds of other candidates who have all the same qualifications. Here are the four secret things that your interviewers will be looking for:

◆ application

◆ attitude

◆ commitment

◆ and enthusiasm.

Being a camera operator can be physically and mentally exhausting, so you must appear to be the sort of person who can work well as part of a team when the going gets tough – *and* still respond to the director's demands, *and* still deal politely yet firmly with difficult artistes or presenters. As one TV boss told me:

> 'You can teach just about anyone to frame a shot, but camera ops need tact, diplomacy and discipline in spade-loads if they're going to be any good at the job.'

So, here are a few things to bear in mind when you're preparing for your interview:

◆ Think about times when you have displayed good team work – perhaps there was a time at college when a project went wrong and you all had to pull together. Jot down some notes about how you coped, and work this story into the conversation.

◆ Show your absolute, rock-solid commitment to being the best camera operator in the industry by talking about your passion for photography, or how you love to video family occasions, or how you made a great film of the school play – though don't sound as though you want to be a director, that will make your interviewers suspicious. You may, one day, want to be a director, but keep that under your hat for now. At this exact moment, they are looking for someone who wants to be a great camera operator and only a great camera operator.

◆ Read Chapter 9, so you understand the importance of health and safety in television. Then work it into the conversation. This will impress your interviewers enormously.

◆ Read as many technical books and magazines as possible, so you can talk knowledgeably about the subject of photography (and be able to answer the 'depth of field' question!).

◆ Watch television analytically so you can discuss your favourite programmes, and say why you enjoyed the camerawork, and lighting. Remember to mention some of the programmes made by the company where you're being interviewed!

◆ Don't worry about being nervous. All good people are nervous.

SOUND

You need the same academic qualifications as a camera operator: aim for three A-levels, and a degree in something like media. Interviewers are also looking for evidence that you can work well as part of a team, but most of all they're looking for someone who just *loves* sound – all sound recordists are hi-fi buffs, it's in their blood. The first thing you should do – after reading this book – is apply to help out on hospital radio. If you can show that you are really committed to making great broadcast sound, you will stand head and shoulders above the other candidates (some of whom, as we discovered earlier, have chosen to specialise in sound because they think it's an easy option).

To prepare for your interview, you should also read as many technical books and magazines as possible, and you should be able to talk about which programmes you enjoy, and why, and you should understand about health and safety (see Chapter 9). But most importantly, you must be able to convey your absolute, copper-bottomed commitment to being the best sound recordist in the known universe.

POST-PRODUCTION

Editing

If you want to edit, you should have worked in an operational edit suite, before you start applying for jobs. Assuming that you can't afford to buy your own, this means doing a media degree, and making sure that you get to use the editing equipment as much as possible (you'll need three decent A-levels to get on a good media course – see Chapter 5). There's one other thing you'll need if you want to be an editor, and that's a very special personality. Because here's the thing about editors: they get cooped up in a tiny, airless room for weeks on end with directors. Directors come in all flavours, from affable to arrogant, and the editor has to be able to get on with every single one of them. This isn't as easy as it sounds; editing is a strangely emotional time for directors. At the beginning it's exciting, because they get to see their rushes after weeks of shooting. Then it's depressing, when they realise that the stuff they actually shot doesn't look anywhere near as good as the stuff they imagined they'd shot.

A good editor should be all these things:

◆ Easy to talk to, and fun to be with – the sort of person you wouldn't mind being cooped up with in an airless room for weeks on end.

◆ Intelligent, sensitive and tactful.

◆ Someone who loves telling stories, which is essentially what editing is all about.

◆ Computer literate and interested in electronics – it's good to have some understanding of the technology.

When you're preparing for your interview, remember that these are the qualities you need to project. You can show your love of story-telling by discussing the kind of programmes you enjoy, and why you enjoy them. Two points to bear in mind here: try to mention at least one programme made by the company that's interviewing you; and never say something like 'I don't watch TV' – interviewers are looking for people with a passion for television.

Before your interview, read every magazine and book about editing that you can get your hands on; you should have a considered opinion about the relative merits of different types of editing suites, and be able to answer questions like: 'What's the difference between linear and non-linear editing?' There are two more questions that pop up regularly at editors' interviews. The first is: 'Which would you rather work on, documentaries or drama?' There is no right answer to this – they're just trying to establish that you've thought abut the different skills needed to work on these two very different types of programmes. The second question is: 'What do you want to be in ten years time?' There is only one possible answer to this one: 'I want to be a great editor.' Practise saying it!

Finally, don't worry if you're nervous on the day – being a bit flustered is an entirely appropriate response when you're being interviewed for the job of your dreams. In fact, it's a good thing. You don't want to come over too cocky, as your interviewers are looking for a nice, sensitive, tactful person.

But do try to have fun – they're also looking for someone who's easy to talk to and get on with.

Dubbing

If you think you'd like to spend your television career in dubbing, you need to convince interviewers of three things:

1. That your ears have great potential.

2. That you're keen to learn a brand new skill, one that few people in the world have mastered.

3. That you are bright enough to understand basic electrical theory.

The first is a tricky one to get across, and certainly being musical will help your chances (most dubbing mixers play an instrument). But as one senior dubbing mixer explained:

> 'Being able to do what we do isn't a natural talent, it's a learned skill. I'm looking for people who are aware of sound, and interested in what sound can do, but whoever gets this job is going to have to learn from scratch, anyway.'

Because of this, he says he likes his trainees fresh from college or university, or even straight from school. Seems you need to train ears when they're young.

Did you panic when you read number three? Don't worry if you didn't do any science at school – you don't need A-level physics to be a dubbing mixer. During your two years' training you will learn enough basic physics to be able to understand why there's a buzz on the line when you plug the microphone in. In fact, there is no one A-level or degree course that will fit you for being a dubbing mixer. There is one quality, though, that marks out all new dubbing trainees, and that's a willingness to learn completely new skills. Oh, and there's one more, very interesting thing to say before we leave the subject of dubbing, and that's how tiring it is. Be warned that learning to use your ears properly – actually *listening* to things, rather than just hearing them – is surprisingly exhausting.

FLOOR/UNIT MANAGING

Floor/unit managers/first assistant directors (or FUMFADs for short) all start as runners, then work up to being thirds, then seconds and firsts. TV bosses are looking for three main qualities in the people they train to become FUMFADs:

◆ A broad education up to at least GCSE standard (but I would aim for a minimum of 3 Cs at A-level, so you have the option of doing a good media degree. Also, the BBC likes its floor managers to have a university education).

◆ Strong communication and organisational skills.

◆ Some proper, paid, experience of either television production, or theatre stage management.

This last point is crucial: you need some real experience in the big wide world before applying for this job. People tend to come at it from two different directions.

Peter is an excellent and much sought after FUMFAD who works on all sorts of big productions. He did a media degree, then worked for a police video department for a couple of years, before getting a runner's job on a network soap, and quickly moving up the ladder to fully-fledged FUMFAD. Then there's Sally, who came up through theatre – she worked as a stage manager in rep for two years, before getting her first runner's job.

In a nutshell, TV bosses are looking for a certain maturity, a certain lived-in feeling to the people they take on to train up as FUMFADs.

'It's not really a job for someone fresh from college, who has no knowledge of real life,' said one boss. 'Trainees need to be able to deal directly with all sorts of people, from cabinet ministers to rock stars. They have to be organised. They have to have strong leadership qualities, yet still be able to take direction. They must be sensitive *and* thick-skinned. Most people need a bit of experience of life under their belts before they can tackle a job like this.'

Of course, there are always exceptions to any rule – if you're naturally mature and organised, you may well be able to talk yourself into a runner's job straight from college. It has been done. But you must be prepared to keep trying. Here's Peter's advice:

'If you think you can do the job, and you believe in yourself, then *don't give up*! I decided I wanted to work for my local television station when I was 15 years old. I wrote scores of letters, and I was interviewed by several people – none of whom, I discovered later, were actually in a position to give me a job. But I did a media course, and got some production experience making videos for the police, and ten years after I first applied, I finally got my first job in the building where I'd always imagined myself working. I still get a buzz every morning when I walk into work. I think of all the times I sat in the reception as a nervous interviewee, and I have to pinch myself because I actually work here now!'

One final note – you will do yourself a big favour by reading Chapter 9 before you go for any interviews. Understanding health and safety is an important part of the FUMFAD's job.

SECRETARIAL/PAs

If your aim is to become a PA, you need to get yourself a job as a production secretary (or production coordinator) first, so you can build up your keyboard skills, and most importantly, learn how to oil the wheels of the television process. Because that's the magic of all good PAs: they know how to get things done, who to talk to, and how to talk to them, so that the production runs smoothly and without a hitch.

But you won't walk straight into a job as a television production secretary, unless you're very lucky, and particularly brilliant. Probably, you'll need to start off in a clerical or secretarial job, and work your way up. Here are the qualifications and qualities you'll need to make it as a PA:

◆ A media degree is a good thing because you'll learn about the industry. You'll need at least 3 Cs at A-level to get on a good media course – see next chapter.

◆ Excellent keyboard skills.

◆ Good communication and organisational qualities.

◆ Numeracy: you must be able to add up quickly and accurately – in minutes and seconds! Think about this for a minute (which is 60 seconds, by the way), it's not like adding up to a hundred; it requires heavy-duty mental arithmetic skills. Try this question: the running time of a VT insert is 5' 14". It's been playing for 2'37". How long is left? Quickly, I need an answer *now* . . .

◆ And, as a bonus, you should be able to count bars of music.

It used to be that would-be production secretaries applied for jobs the normal way: by sending in their CVs to personnel, and waiting for a post to become available. But the other day I heard a story that shows how things are changing. I pass it on to you to think about, and perhaps act upon.

The head of regional programmes at one of the network companies was trawling through his in-tray, filled, as usual, with letters from wannabe researchers, when he discovered a letter from a feisty young thing who wanted to be a production secretary. She had watched all his programmes and written an excellent letter detailing why she wanted to work on them. Intrigued, he interviewed her, found that she had all the requisite qualities and qualifications to make a good production secretary, plus the bonus of a great sense of humour. He hired her.

If you fancy taking the direct approach, my advice would be to pick a department, like regional programmes, or documentaries, and write to the head of that department, rather than targeting individual producers.

One final tip: there are two excellent websites which can help you find your first job – www.skillset.org, and www.skillsformedia.com. They offer information on what jobs and training courses are available right now, and they'll also help with individual careers advice.

5

Getting onto a Media Course

First, a potted history of media courses. They appeared in the late seventies, grew popular in the eighties, and by the nineties, every sort of media course was hugely over-subscribed. New ones sprang up all over the country, but not all of them were well-equipped or even well-thought-through. By the late nineties, media courses had developed a bad reputation. Newspapers wrote critical articles about them. Eminent educationalists pronounced them 'a short cut to the dole queue'. And everyone else made bad jokes, like: 'What do you say to a media studies graduate? Burger and fries, please!'

Then something interesting happened, something which perhaps should have happened earlier: television got involved in the shaping of media courses. TV bosses visited the colleges and universities and said: 'This is what we want – teach this, in this way, with this equipment.' The good courses pretty smartly cottoned on, and developed their syllabus accordingly (the very good ones were already doing useful work). TV companies began to forge links with colleges that were teaching good and useful stuff, and soon the companies were giving most of their work experience places to these hand-picked, industry-approved colleges. And so it came to pass that a two-tier system of media courses developed: excellent, well-respected courses that were geared to meet the needs of the industry. And other ones. You need to know how to find the former, and avoid the latter.

KNOWING THE DIFFERENCE BETWEEN MEDIA AND MEDIA STUDIES

But first, a quick digression – what's the difference between media and media studies? 'Media studies' is a purely academic degree, where you analyse media in all its forms: if you want to study the media's role in modern society, or debate the symbolism of soaps, then media studies is for you. 'Media', or 'media production', on the other hand, is a completely different sort of degree, which should teach you professional skills like how to make television programmes. If you want to work in cameras, sound or post-production, a media degree from an industry-approved university or college will stand you in good stead. It's a useful degree if you want to floor manage, depending on what you plan to do the year after college (see Chapter 4). And it's useful if you want to be a researcher – as long as you're aware of how some producers feel about media degrees (see Chapter 3).

FINDING A GOOD COURSE

So how do you go about finding out which are the good, industry-approved courses? Start with a list of universities where you'd like to study. (The Skillset website is a good research tool. It has links to other useful sites – like skillsformedia, and the British Film Institute – where you can find details of all the media courses in the UK.) Then interview the course providers until you have a shortlist of courses that are worth visiting. Here are the questions to ask:

◆ **Do you have industry links?** If the answer is yes, ask which TV companies they have links with. And if you really want to do your research thoroughly, phone the TV companies to check (ask for someone in personnel or training, they'll be happy to help). Some television companies proudly announce their media course links on their websites.

◆ **How much hands-on, practical work do you do?** The right answer is at least 50 per cent. You need to know that your course will give you a good grounding in practical skills like how to edit, or how to operate a camera, as well as covering the theory side of things.

◆ **What sort of facilities do you have?** You need to know that your course has industry-standard editing equipment, and enough cameras to cover every student's coursework needs. Some courses even have their own cable television stations. A good course will be pleased to boast about its facilities, and happy to show you round.

◆ **How much help do you give in finding work experience placements?** Good courses will give you lots of help and advice; some will even organise the whole thing for you. If the course organisers are cagey about discussing work experience, be suspicious.

◆ **How many of the staff have worked in television?** It has to be a good thing if some of the course tutors have worked – or are still working – in the industry.

◆ **What kind of jobs do your graduates get?** Some courses specialise in producing technical graduates; others tend to turn out wannabe producers and directors. If you know you want to be a camera operator one day, it's worth applying to courses with a technical bent.

When you visit, talk to as many lecturers and technical support staff as you can, to get a feel for the place. What you're looking for is enthusiasm – if staff love what they do, they'll teach you well and you'll have fun learning.

It's sometimes surprising which courses come up trumps. You'll find good ones tucked away in all sorts of unusual places. For instance, Bournemouth University runs a three-year degree course that has an outstanding reputation. Another well-respected course is run by East Coast Media out of the old fishing town of Grimsby on the Lincolnshire coast. And tucked away in the suburbs of Leeds, the University College of Trinity and All Saints offers an excellent media course, which produces top-quality graduates.

Examining what makes a good course

So why do these ones work? It's worth examining a good course in detail. Let's take Bournemouth as the benchmark. Here's what's good about it:

◆ Students do a lot of group work, which is great training for real life. Television is a team sport.

◆ The industry-standard equipment is professionally organised and managed: students have to book out camera and sound equipment through the technical support department. (Again, just like real life.) And there's plenty of equipment, so everyone gets hands-on experience.

◆ Students learn how to write scripts and tell stories. Understanding how to put a script together is one of the most important TV skills. Storytelling is what television is all about – whatever TV job you want to do, it's an important skill to learn.

◆ Students have to specialise for their final year project: they decide whether they're going to be an editor, a producer, or a production manager, or whatever. This might not be the job they end up doing in the real world, but it's good practice for them to see a job through.

◆ And finally, perhaps the most important point about this course is that it instills in its students a certain humility: graduates don't expect to walk into a top job straight from college. They understand that their degree is only the very beginning, and they'll need to start as runners or junior researchers and work their way up, just like everyone else.

WHAT QUALIFICATIONS WILL YOU NEED?

If you do decide to do media as a degree, you'll need at least 3 Cs at A-level to get on a worthwhile course. The more popular the course, the higher the qualifications (Bournemouth's BATV requires a minimum of 3 Bs). Course organisers are looking for a broad education. The Dean of one of the best ones sums it up: 'We want well-rounded people with varied interests and a passion for telling stories.'

Because the good degree courses are oversubscribed, you'll be expected to work for your place: some courses will put you through a tough interview, others will ask you to produce written work, or even a video, to back up your application.

One day, all media courses will be good, and all media students will be justly proud of their hard-earned degrees. There's talk of 'kite-marking' courses, and other ways of giving official recognition to centres of excellence. Until then, you need to do your own research.

Part 3
Doing The Job

'Getting your foot in the door is just the first step. Being successful at creating great TV takes time, effort and above all dedication.'

Patrick Titley, Senior Producer/Director

6

Working as a Researcher

Working as a researcher is different from any other television job in one very important way: researchers help create things for the other people to do. If you're on cameras or sound – or a floor manager on a studio-based show – you come on board once the programme has been shaped and the scripts have been written; it's your job to bring the programme to life. But a researcher starts with a blank page. For this reason alone, working as a researcher is thrilling and terrifying, in equal measures.

I remember when the enormity of this concept dawned on me. I was a baby researcher on a Yorkshire Television regional programme called *Calendar Calling*. It was a great show in its day: we would go to some village in the middle of nowhere, and capture the eccentricities of the community in a glorious half-hour of local programming. For reasons I never quite understood, we didn't just take a film crew, we took an entire outside broadcast unit. An OB unit is really quite something to behold, and back then it was like an army rolling into town: three enormous trucks, scores of riggers and electricians and props people, six camera operators, boom operators, and van-loads of other people who seemed to have important things to do.

I had set up for us to shoot a 'well-dressing' ceremony in a sweet little Derbyshire village – roses round the doors, thatched roofs, tiny twisting lanes – where, once a year, everyone in the village would get together to decorate the village well in flowers; hence 'well-dressing'. (I seem to remember it was a thank-you ceremony, because the well had saved villagers from the plague 400 years earlier. Or something like that.)

Fast forward to early morning on the day of the shoot. I'm standing in the buttery sunshine of the village square, listening to birdsong and watching the villagers at work, congratulating myself on the lovely programme we're about to make. Then the OB unit rolls in. Truck after truck. Van after van. Cables everywhere. Mess. Noise. Broken paving slabs.

One by one, the villagers dropped their floral tributes and stared, astonished at the circus unfolding in front of them. And I thought: 'I am responsible for this.' It was a salutary moment.

Try to hold that thought, because later on in this chapter we'll look at the responsibility of programme makers: how to treat people, and how to do your job without causing good people distress, damage or any other sort of upset. But first, let's consider the other big difference between working as a researcher and doing any other television job. Camera operators, sound recordists, editors, PAs and floor managers are all trained before they're expected to be able to do the job. But most researchers get thrown right in at the deep end, where they either sink or swim. Here's a guide to staying afloat – a look at the things you may be expected to do when your get your first job as a researcher.

PRE-PRODUCTION

Having ideas

Whatever research job you get you'll be expected to contribute ideas, and by their worth shall you be judged. Producers just love researchers with ideas. People who don't work in television always ask: 'Where do ideas come from?'. A friend of mine tells them they come from a special book.

But here's the secret of where ideas really come from – from everywhere. They're all around you: on the television or radio, in newspapers and magazines, on advertising hoardings, in the music charts, in books, and in the conversations you have with your friends. Starting from now, you need to train yourself to look for ideas that will be talking points, because that's what makes a good story – one that's worth repeating. Be open to new experiences, and think about things that are happening in the world. Good ideas come to people who ask questions like: 'How does that work?', 'Why does that happen?', and 'How do they do that?'.

Keeping an ideas file

I'm going to pass onto you the best bit of advice I was ever given on how to have ideas: keep an 'ideas file'. All good producers and researchers have one. Some keep notes of carefully thought-out ideas and lists of contact numbers, others have an old dog-eared folder stuffed with cuttings ripped from newspapers and magazines. However you do it, just do it. Then, every time you start on a new project, trawl the ideas file to see if there's anything pertinent.

Sometimes, the best ideas come from the synergy of a production meeting, when everyone gets together to pitch in thoughts. At times like this, don't just sit there, *say something!* Researchers who say nothing at meetings are generally mistrusted: colleagues think that they've got nothing to say because they're a bit dim. Or even worse, that they're being precious with their ideas, jealously guarding them to use at a later time. Always be generous with your ideas. There are plenty more where they came from, and the truth is that the more ideas you give away, the more you'll have. Besides, an idea shared is an idea improved, and the more people who have ownership of an idea, the better. Say you're at a meeting to come up with ideas for a new sports show. One person says: 'How about an item on skate-boarding, it's getting big again?'. Someone else says: 'I read a piece about people who're using big kites to pull the skateboards.' A third person chips in: 'I read that too, it was Bristol, wasn't it?' Someone else says: 'We could set up a record attempt – the biggest kite ever to pull a skateboard, or biggest number of skateboarders to be pulled by kites. Bristol Downs would be a good location.' And so on . . .

So who has ownership of that idea? It was a team effort, and that's a good thing because it means that everyone on the team is behind the idea. But if you were the researcher who made the first suggestion, you could be extra proud of your-self – you sparked a good discussion, which produced a good story.

Getting passionate

There's one more tip about having ideas, which may seem blindingly obvious, but I'm going to say it anyway: know and love your subject. May you always work on programmes dealing with something that you're passionate about. It's so much easier to come up with great ideas when you know your subject inside out. You may be lucky, and sail through your career working only on programmes that delight you. But more than likely, you'll have to research subjects that definitely do not float your boat. There's only one thing to do in this situation: *make* yourself passionate! I can think of at least a couple of times when I've researched subjects that I didn't find the least bit interesting (for the record, they were farming and computers). So I did what I had to do – I immersed myself completely. For the farming programme I got up at dawn every day to listen to the early morning farming show on the radio. I subscribed to *Farmer's Weekly*. I made friends with the local farmers' union representative, and visited farms and cattle markets. And do you know what – I loved it! Soon, I found farming just the most fascinating thing ever (I still can't get excited about computers, though . . .).

How to tell if your idea is any good

Eventually your idea detector will become so finely tuned that you'll be able to sniff out a good one at 20 paces. But until then, here's a surefire way to tell if your idea for a story, or a programme, or a series, is a good one: ask yourself, does it stand up to the Vest Test? Nothing to do with old-fashioned underwear; it's a simple four-part test to tell if your idea has legs.

◆ **'V for Visual:** Imagine your idea in pictures – what will it look like? This may sound like an obvious thing to do – television being a visual medium – but you'd be surprised how many people get carried away with an idea without thinking through the visuals. Try to think what locations you'd need to tell the story, and what the action would look like. If there's an interviewee, think what she could be doing while she's talking. The best story in the world won't work on television unless you have something interesting for viewers to look at.

◆ **'E' for Emotion:** Will your idea provoke an emotion – any emotion: fear, sadness, excitement, happiness, compassion, envy, wonder, recognition? A good story or programme should make you *feel* something. Envy, in the best sense of the word, can make for excellent programming (*'Oooh, I would love that car, or that dress, or that house or that holiday . . .'*). Happy television is always watchable: comedy stirs the senses and makes you feel good, and everyone loves the glow you get from a happy ending. Fear, sadness and excitement keep you glued to the screen, to find out what happens next. Recognition makes you feel involved because it has a resonance of your own life: it provokes a kind of *'yes, I feel like that too'*, or *'I worry that will happen to me'* sort of feeling.

◆ **'S' for Surprise:** Programmes with the *'gee whiz, I never knew that!'* factor are always good. We all love to be told exciting stories about why things are and how things work. It needn't be a completely original thought (television has few of those), but it's a good story if it tells you something unexpected, in an unexpected way.

◆ **'T' for Topical:** If it's in the news, it's at the front of people's minds, and therefore it's a subject that will get people talking. Lots of television programmes – from consumer shows to daytime programmes, to children's magazine shows – feed on topical ideas: the unseasonable weather; the split of a girl band; or a new movie release that's causing controversy. Topical is just another word for gossip, and everyone loves gossip. In TV news a 'good story' is deemed to be one that everyone will be talking about down the pub that night. In children's programmes, a good story is one that all the kids will be talking about in the playground next day. Do you see a theme developing?

If your idea has a V, an E, an S or a T, it has a good chance of working. If it has all four, you're a genius.

Budgets

There is one more thing to talk about before we leave the subject of ideas, and that's the horrible reality of budgets. As a researcher, you won't be in charge of a programme budget, but it's everyone's responsibility to make sure there are no drastic overspends, so your ideas should be practical. The basic rule is, beware of actors, archive, movies and music, and not necessarily in that order. Once you enter the territory of copyright and contracts, you're in a dangerous minefield, and you could end up horribly maimed, with your budget blown to smithereens. And the producer will hate you. In a perfect world, all your ideas will be brilliant and cheap, but if you do need to dabble in the above, check out Chapter 8 for detailed information on copyright and other tricky stuff.

Setting up stories

Finding contributors and locations is called 'setting up' a story. If you love the thrill of the chase, you'll have a lot of fun doing this part of the job. It's a bit like being a detective: there's lots of finding-out and tracking-down to do, and you must be thorough and dogged in your approach. It's important to get as much right at this stage as possible. This is cheap time, because it just involves you – once you get a crew or editor involved, you're into premium time. Mistakes made during the setting-up process will need to be sorted during the shoot, or in post-production. This will cost the production money, and ruin your reputation. And as we've already established, producers don't like researchers who cost them extra money.

Finding people and places

The internet is a fantastic research tool. If you're looking for an expert, or a good quote, Google (or a similar search engine) is a great place to start. But there are two problems with internet research. First, you'll be overwhelmed with information. Say you're looking for a child psychologist. Type 'child psychology' in the search box, and watch what happens: thousands of results. You could spend the next three days trawling through the information, and still not find what you're looking for. Much better, then, to locate the homepage for the British Psychological Society – phone them, and ask their press liaison person for some recommendations. It's always better to talk to a real, live human being. All universities and most organisations have a homepage, complete with a list of contact numbers. Online magazines are a good resource: make friends with the editor, and you might get access to his specialist knowledge as well as his contacts book.

The second problem with the internet is its democratic nature – anyone can publish anything, so your search will bring up academic papers as well as wild conspiracy theories. Always check every piece of information you download. Remember, the internet is only a tool, and like all tools, you have to know how to use it.

Stage one
Let's take an example of a story that was set up using the internet – remember that rodeo story I told you about in Chapter 1, The Story of a Shoot? I was looking for some very specific things:

◆ A family who lived within a couple of hours' drive of New Orleans, who were nuts about rodeo.

◆ The children had to be the right age for our audience to identify with (10-17).

◆ The location had to look good, and also be a safe environment for the presenter to learn rodeo skills.

◆ Finally, we had to be satisfied that the animals were loved and well-cared for.

So, how would you go about finding this mythical family? The first thing to do is to search the net, because it's a cheap way to do research. I typed in 'Louisiana Rodeo', and eventually ended up at a home page run by a bunch of rodeo kids down in the far south-west of Louisiana. And hallelujah, there was an e-mail address. I became cyber-pen-pals with a teenage girl, who gave me her dad's e-mail address at work – he organised rodeos all over the state. I told him what I was looking for and he said he'd help. But he went quiet for too long, so I had to put stage two into action, and spend some money.

Stage two

Stage two involved going to the library and asking for help. I was working for Yorkshire Television at the time, and they have the most marvellous library. (A note about libraries: if you're working for one of the big network companies, or the BBC, it's worth getting to know the librarians. They are clever people who are wizards at finding information.) Like all good TV librarians, the YTV people have access to an information search tool called *Nexis*. It's a worldwide service which tracks newspaper and magazine articles from all over the world – from *Newsweek* and *The New York Times* to tiny local papers in the middle of nowhere. (You have to pay, but it's worth every penny.)The search turned up several articles about kid rodeo stars, one of which mentioned a rodeo class in the Baton Rouge area. Getting warm! I phoned the arena mentioned in the piece, and got an ex-directory phone number for the man who ran the classes. He turned out to be a great character, with two teenage kids – both rodeo champions – and a backyard kitted out like a real rodeo ring. Eureka!!! Two days later, the 'e-mail man' who'd gone quiet got back in touch, with the same phone number. Bad luck, but you can't hang around waiting forever.

The snowball effect

Once you've made one good contact, he should put you in touch with other people you need to talk to. It's a kind of snowball effect. I had the distinction of being the person who had to find some naked people for the UK's first ever all-naked game show (I can tell you're impressed). I had 24 hours to discover whether the show had legs (if you pardon the anatomical pun), and whether enough naturists could be persuaded to take part in it. My first port of call was a naturist home page run by a retired military chap who spent his golden years wandering around in the buff, somewhere in the south of England. I talked to him, explained the show – which was to be a sort of naked *Indiana Jones and the Temple of Doom,* if you can imagine such a concept – and asked him if he would care to take part. He gracefully declined (probably a good move), but put me in touch with dozens of other naturists who would be delighted to appear on national TV, naked as the day they were born.

Making that first call: how to persuade people to help you

The first time you contact someone will probably be on the phone, and the tone of your voice will influence how they react to you. Don't be embarrassed, tentative or apologetic, but equally don't come over all cocky and pushy like a double glazing salesman. Before you dial the number, take some deep breaths, think positive thoughts, and *smile.* Take care to sound sensible, intelligent, and most importantly, enthusiastic. If you think that the programme you're calling about is the best idea in the world, and a really worthwhile piece of television, your callee will too, because enthusiasm is infectious, and almost always charming.

Don't be put off if the person at the other end sounds harassed or grumpy – you've been psyching yourself up to make this call, but they weren't expecting it. Suggest that you call back at a better time, or say that you'll fax a request through first, so they can consider your needs before you call back, and a set time and date to make the next phone call. Sometimes this is a good idea anyway, especially if your request is a complicated one; it gives people time to take in the information before you bombard them with questions. And it's always a good idea to follow up with a fax or e-mail anyway, confirming your conversation – it lets people know you're serious, and it ensures that they have the details written down.

Looking after contributors

Once someone has agreed to be on your programme, you have to make them your friend (unless, of course, you're working on an investigative programme that aims to expose the corrupt and the criminal). This sounds awful – really callous and calculating – but it's true. It's your job to make sure that people don't back out at the last minute, leaving the production in the lurch. One of the best ways of doing this is to make sure they have some sort of relationship with you.

The relationship side of things can go a bit awry sometimes, as some people persist in getting hold of the wrong end of the stick if you show any interest in them.

A young, very attractive researcher came to grief over this, when she was working on a religious programme. She had to contact a particular celebrity – an aging sex-symbol-rock'n'roll-star-turned-actor-type, who shall remain nameless, but he knows who he is – to get him on the programme to talk about his spiritual views. It was a delicate subject, so they had many phone calls, and by the time he turned up at the studio, he had decided he was in love with her. Her producer was unsympathetic to the poor girl's plight, implying that she had somehow led him on. But, as she lamented later, still deeply shocked: 'I was only doing my job!'.

There are worse things than being hit on by aging celebrities. At some point in your career you'll have to cope with real people, who are struggling with real emotions.

One of my first jobs as a researcher was to make a film about the work of a hospital baby heart-surgery unit. I had to find families whose children had been saved by the unit, some who were still waiting for surgery, and some whose babies had died. The hospital put me in touch with one woman – well, girl actually, she was only 19 – whose baby had died on the operating table. She was an unmarried mother, living hundreds of miles from her family, and she was emotionally very raw. I went to see her a few times, we struck up a relationship, and she agreed to be interviewed because she thought it would be a cathartic experience. It turned out to be a bad decision on her part. She fell apart just thinking about the filming, and really went to pieces on camera. My producer was delighted – he thought this made wonderful television – but I thought the interview was embarrassing and intrusive. And after we'd packed up and gone off to the next location, she really cracked up. I got a call that night at midnight, and spent several hours consoling her on the phone. She rang almost every night for at least a week, just needing someone to talk to. I got in touch with the hospital chaplain, and he arranged some counselling for her, but for months she would still call me when she went through a bad patch.

Alice is a researcher who's worked on documentaries dealing with all sorts of difficult subjects. Here's what she had to say about the researcher-contributor relationship:

Very often, the people you've persuaded to take part in your programme didn't really want anything to do with it – they only agreed because you talked them into it. So it's your duty to protect them.

And she added this warning about finding contributors for programmes dealing with sensitive subjects like, say, anorexia, or alcoholism:

'Sometimes taking part in a programme can stir up bad emotions for people – they're coping okay until you come along with the cameras, then they go to pieces. So you've got to be there for them. It can be a 24-hour job – you can't just switch your phone off at 6 o'clock and go to the bar.'

Take these stories as a warning if you like, but don't let them stop you trying to have a good friendship with the people you have on your programmes – contributors need to feel that they can trust and confide in someone, and you are that someone. Friendship is a two-way thing; once you have struck up a relationship with your interviewees, it's your job to make sure that they are not damaged by the experience. Most people are straightforward and fun to get to know, and it's a privilege to be allowed into their lives. Don't ever abuse that privilege.

What to check

Quite simply, everything you can think of! It's a good idea to write yourself a check list before you call – just headlines to jog your memory – because people will get fed up if you start calling them every day with the lame excuse: 'Oh, I just forgot to ask . . .'. I found the following in one of my old notebooks. The story was about Double Dutch rope-jumping in New York. Double Dutch is fancy skipping which would knock your socks off. It came to New York hundreds of years ago with the Dutch settlers, and since has become a street game, particularly popular with African-Americans. Lately it's become a serious sport with strict rules and regulations. I'd already established the shooting date in an earlier phone call, so these were the things I needed to check:

What's the location? Describe. Will there be lots of people around?

How many girls in a team?

How old are the girls, roughly?

Who's the fastest? What's the record?

Will you bring the ropes?

Will they be wearing uniforms — what colours?

Will you bring refreshments for the girls?

Will you be able to teach the presenter to do something simple, so she can join in?

What should the presenter wear?

Will you show us how you develop a new freestyle move?

Will one of the girls be able to explain the differences between the different styles?

Why don't boys do it?

Will there be music – can they do it without!!!!

Pretty obvious questions really.

◆ You can check what the location looks like at the recce – we'll look at the importance of recces later in this chapter – but it helps to imagine the location when you're trying to think of ways to write up the story.

◆ It's also worth knowing whether you're going to be shooting in a busy street or a quiet park where no one will bother you.

◆ You need to have an idea of how many people you're dealing with, and whether the set-up will be manageable.

◆ Also whether you're expected to bring any props, or feed and water the contributors.

◆ If you have a presenter, it's worth checking what she will be able to do, so she doesn't just stand around like a spare part.

◆ It's always good to ask what people will be wearing: tight checks or stripes or chevrons can look awful, and as a rule white shirts make things difficult for the cameraman, because if he exposes for the bright white shirt, the rest of the picture will look too dark.

◆ And always, always, ask about music, especially on a story like this!

The money question

I didn't mention money in the example above, because I never do – it's best not to put ideas into people's heads. As a rule, there will be nothing in the budget to pay people a contribution fee, not nowadays, although you should always cover their expenses, and it's good PR to bring coffee and biscuits and generally look after the people who are taking part. But it's a sad fact of life that the world is closing up, and more and more people expect to be paid for taking part in a television programme. If someone has money on their mind, they will ask; it's then up to you to negotiate with the producer how much you can afford to pay them.

Interestingly, the guy who was in charge of the Double Dutch team did ask for money, and he waited until the recce to spring it on me. Like a lot of people, he assumed that television producers have loads of spare money, but they're just too mean to hand it over to contributors. So he waited until the producer and I met him on the recce before he made his demands, presumably on the assumption that we had crossed the Atlantic to do the story, and we couldn't go home empty handed. It was a tricky negotiation because, to his mind, we had come from England to film him, therefore we must work on a production with a fairly big budget, and he wanted some of that budget for his girls (actually, he wanted quite a lot of it). I would gladly have given him money – he did great work with underprivileged teenagers – but what he didn't realise was that we could only afford to film in New York because we had pared the budget to the bone (and we were shooting six stories in four days!). In the end, we squeezed a couple of hundred pounds out of somewhere for him, but he felt cheated, and the producer and I felt mean.

But what happens if someone goes through with filming, then demands money afterwards; even going as far as to threaten an injunction on his interview? This is a tricky area. It's always a good idea to get a contributor to sign a consent form before you film him – in fact, some television companies insist that *all* interviewees sign consent forms – but that's not always practical. And some people believe that consent forms are unnecessary anyway: if a contributor allows you to point a camera at him, and goes through with the whole filming process, he has given implied consent, which he can't just withdraw on a whim. Besides, unless money changes hands, the consent form isn't worth the paper it's written on. You need to pay someone a fee before a written agreement like this becomes a legal document.

If you're really worried that someone will wriggle out of your spoken deal at a later date, there are two things to do:

a) Put something in writing: a letter confirming all the arrangements, with an extra sentence to the effect: 'I'm so sorry we can't pay you a fee for all your help, but our budget just won't stretch to paying contributors . . .' The good thing is, you'll be legally bullet-proof; the danger is that you put ideas in their heads about payment.

b) Contract them through your company's legal department, paying them a token fee. This would be a good idea if the interview was a controversial one, and you suspected that the interviewee might get cold feet at a later date. It might also be a good idea to contract anyone whom you suspect may chicken out of filming, or get a better offer. No one can argue with a contract. And sometimes you may want to contract contributors to protect them. We contracted the contestants who took part in the all-naked game show, so that they had some protection from other television shows, that could have tried to use clips of the programme out of context.

Writing a script

Scriptwriting is a skill that every researcher needs – more and more programmes use presenters, and presenter-led stories nearly always need scripts. If you can write a good script, you will soon become the producer's favourite researcher. There are four types of scene you can use in a presenter-led script:

1. **PTCs. A PTC** is a **piece to camera,** where the presenter talks directly to the camera.

2. **V/Os – voice-overs.** These are bits of commentary script where the presenter talks over footage, out of vision. They're often recorded later, at the dubbing stage.

3. **Interviews.**

4. **Unscripted presenter action.** This is often the best part of a story – you put the presenter in an interesting situation, then sit back and watch what happens.

It's up to you to weave these four types of scene together to tell your story. Think of your script as a symphony with four possible movements, and vary the pace and tone by shifting from one type of scene to another. Say you're writing a script for a holiday show about a little town in Portugal. You'd probably start with a piece to camera from your presenter. Then you'd go to a sequence of holidaymakers having fun, with a bit of voice-over explaining what sort of people would enjoy a holiday in this particular spot, and maybe a bit of information about the area. Then you'd cut back to your presenter doing something visually interesting – perhaps splashing in the village fountain with some local children. Then perhaps you'd cut to an interview with a happy holidaymaker. And so on . . .

Everyone finds writing scripts difficult at first, because they all make the same mistake – they don't think the story through, *before* they sit down to write it. They've done all the research, and they want to cram every bit of information into the piece, so their story goes something like this: 'and then . . . and then . . . and then.' This is a terrible way to write scripts. What you leave out is just as important as what you put into a story; a good script uses words sparingly. Here's a failsafe way to make sure that your script flows effortlessly:

◆ Think of your script as a story.

◆ Tell the story to a friend. This will give you the spine of the story, and let you know which are the important parts – it will also prove to you how easy it is to tell the story. All you need to do now is write it down!

◆ Block out your story, either on paper or in your head. This means deciding where you're going with the piece – every story needs a strong beginning, an interesting middle bit, and a satisfying ending.

◆ Keep it simple. You may think you're writing the most fascinating script ever produced, but it's no use to anyone if it's crammed full of complicated facts. Before you write your script, read your notes through once, then put them aside and don't look at them again: if you can't understand and recall the information, how do you expect the viewers to grasp it when they hear it for the very first time? (For this reason, big numbers should be avoided.)

◆ When you've finished your script, put it in a drawer overnight, and look at it again the next morning when your mind is fresh. Your first reaction is the right one – if you think it needs more work, it does!

Bearing all that in mind, here's a version of the script for that holiday show story about the town in Portugal. What do you think of this?

(THE PRESENTER IS STANDING ON THE SEA FRONT LOOKING OUT TO SEA. SHE TURNS TO CAMERA)

GLAMOROUS PRESENTER:
Welcome to Porta Marina on the south-east tip of the Portuguese Algarve, a picturesque town that was founded in 1323 by Moorish invaders, and flourished as a fishing port in the sixteenth century. In the eighteenth century, the town became infamous as the place where English artistocratic families sent ignoble noblemen who had disgraced the family name.

(CUT TO PRESENTER AT CAFE TABLE, SURROUNDED BY TOURISTS EATING AND DRINKING)

GLAMOROUS PRESENTER:
Today it's a popular holiday destination,

mainly with British and German tourists, who travel here predominantly to savour the area's famous seafood.

(CUT TO PRESENTER IN FISH MARKET)

GLAMOROUS PRESENTER:
This is Porta Marina's fish market, where the selection of fish available is overwhelming. I'm going to try some of the sardines for which this region is justly famous . . .

Yes, you're right, that's a terrible script. Everything is wrong with it. It's flabby, over-written, and boring. The opening piece to camera is ridiculous. Even assuming that a presenter could remember all that information, and present it in a meaningful way (which is unlikely), it's too early in the story to introduce all that history – nobody cares at this stage. It's just a gabble of impenetrable prose. And the words are all wrong: a script should sound like normal conversation, and people just don't say things like 'ignoble noblemen' or 'predominantly' or 'justly famous' in normal conversation. Nor, for that matter, do you say things like 'impenetrable prose' – what works in print doesn't necessarily work on television. Just try saying 'impenetrable prose' out loud.

There's one more big mistake in this script – the presenter talks to camera in every scene. This is bad because it makes her jump around from one location to another; much more elegant to allow a bit of voice over in between pieces to camera. Also, the viewers will get fed up looking at her if she appears in *every* scene, no matter how glamorous she is.

Let's take the same information, and try the script again.

(THE GLAMOUROUS PRESENTER IS STANDING AT THE QUAYSIDE. A ROPE LANDS AT HER FEET. SHE TAKES IT AND TIES IT ROUND A METAL POST WHILE SHE TALKS)

GLAMOROUS PRESENTER:
You might think that Porta Marina is an unusual place to come on your holidays. . .

(WE CUT TO AN OVER-THE-SHOULDER SHOT TO SEE THAT SHE HAS TETHERED A SMALL FISHING BOAT. THE FISHERMEN ON BOARD WAVE THEIR THANKS. CUT TO TIGHTER SHOT OF PRESENTER)

GLAMOROUS PRESENTER:
It's a working fishing port, and there's not a beach, or a water park, or a shopping mall, for miles around.

(CUT TO MONTAGE OF SHOTS AROUND TOWN – TOURISTS EATING, SHOPPING ETC)

GLAMOROUS PRESENTER V/O:
But this is Portugal's new family holiday hotspot. Here's why . . .

(CUT TO PRESENTER AT TABLE EATING FISHY MEAL)

GLAMOROUS PRESENTER:
For a start, there's the fish – the people of Porta Marina know how to catch fish, and they know how to cook it. The food here is fabulous, and amazingly cheap!

(SHE TUCKS INTO HER MEAL)

(CUT TO SHOTS OF HOLIDAY COMPLEX, WITH KIDS ENJOYING THEMSELVES IN THE POOLS)

GLAMOROUS PRESENTER V/O:
Then there's the accommodation. These old farm buildings have been turned into villa complexes, complete with their own pools. There are several places like this, scattered around the outskirts of Porta Marina – and they're perfect for families with young children.

(CUT TO SHOTS OF PRESENTER WITH LOCAL CHILDREN, SPLASHING IN FOUNTAIN IN TOWN SQUARE)

GLAMOROUS PRESENTER:
But best of all, there's the people of Porta Marina. They really want you to come here, and share their town with them.

(SHE SPLASHES KIDS, AND THEY
START WATER FIGHT. SHE GETS
SOAKED)

That's much better, for three important reasons:

◆ It has a point to it – this is an unusual place to come on
your holidays – and this point gives the story a spine. The
first script was just a forest of information, but the second
one has a path through the forest, so everything is easier
to understand.

◆ It sounds like normal conversation; like something your
friend would tell you. It's fine to put history into the
piece, but you need to do it later on in the story, once
you've given the viewer a feel for what the story is
about. And if you do want to include the stuff about the
Moors and the ignoble noblemen, you must illustrate
the information, by showing shots of interesting Moorish
architecture, or by visiting the tea houses where the
disgraced British aristocracy used to hang out.

◆ It flows much more elegantly because there's some
breathing space between the presenter scenes; she
doesn't jump around all over the place.

By the way, if you like the sound of Porta Marina so much
that you want to go there on holiday, then I have a confession to make – I made it up. Sorry.

Writing a treatment
If you don't need a script, you certainly need a treatment. A
treatment is just an outline of the story you're going to

shoot: a rough draft on paper of where you see your story going. Think of it as a script without the speaking words. Whatever sort of programme you're working on, you should always write a treatment – it concentrates the mind. Remember, research time is cheap, but shooting time and editing time are expensive, so it's mad to go out and shoot lots of stuff and try to make the story work in the edit.

Writing briefing notes

Some producers like to write their own scripts and treatments, in which case you'll be asked to provide briefing notes, which means producing a clear, easy-to-read version of your research notes. This should include contact details for all your interviewees (so that someone else can get in touch with them if necessary) and a bit of background on their personalities, and how you think they'll cope during the shoot. Keep briefs simple and short.

THE SHOOT

Why recces are vital

The preliminary research work is done, and it's time to nail things down, ready for the shoot. It's time for the recce. Recce is short for reconnaissance, which is an army term. A television shoot has much in common with a military campaign: it must be planned in exhaustive detail; and everyone should follow every order immediately, and without a word of argument. Or at least that's what most directors would have you believe... You may have to do your recce alone, or you may get to take a director along with you. But you should never plan a shoot without doing a recce, unless you're working on news, or an undercover documentary, or some other special circumstance. Here's why:

◆ You need to check that your interviewees are happy with the arrangements, and that they understand what's going to happen – this is much easier to do face-to-face than on the phone. And it's easier to build a relationship with someone you've actually met.

◆ You must check directions to the location(s) well in advance of the shoot day, so you can produce a 'call sheet'. A call sheet has directions, maps, lists of contacts and times to RV (rendevous on location) and WRAP (finish for the day. TV legend has it that WRAP stands for 'wind reels and print', something that early movie directors used to say. It's a cute story, but probably WRAP just means 'wrap it up for the day'.) Without good directions, your crew will turn up late, and you will lose valuable shooting time. The best-thought-out, most wonderful story in the world is no use to anyone if there isn't a crew there to film it.

◆ You need to check parking for the crew and production. If the crew can't get parked, ditto the above.

◆ You must check that there's somewhere nearby where the crew can get coffee, or lunch, and take a toilet break. It's amazing how many new researchers forget about the needs of the crew. Researchers only get out filming now and again, so it's an exciting time for them – who needs lunch! But crews do long days every day, and they need to be looked after properly if they're going to do good work.

- If you're shooting indoors, you need to check that there are plenty of electric sockets, so the crew can plug in lights if necessary.

- You need to check the location(s) for strange noises: is there a generator nearby? Is the location on a flight path? Is it next to a building site? (A confession: in my time as a researcher, I have failed to notice all these things on recces.)

- You should check if the crew will need special equipment: for example, if the camera is going to be a long way away from the action, you'll probably need walkie-talkies. Also check if the crew will need special clothing – will the location be very muddy, or very hot and humid?

- You need to check what time things happen: if you're shooting at a school, what time is break? If you're shooting at a factory, what time does the shift change? If you're shooting on a beach, what time does the tide come in?

- And finally, you need to start thinking about pictures, so you can bring your script to life. Everyone has different views on the subject, but I like to do the recce once I've written a draft script, so I know what I'm looking for – it concentrates the mind, and gives you a plan. You can re-write the script when you've done your recce.

Dealing with directors and presenters

Directors and presenters have the sharp-end jobs. The director has to drive the shoot, which is exhausting. And the presenter knows that every time she fluffs her lines, everybody on the crew takes a sharp intake of breath, and mentally shakes his head. With this in mind, make it your job to look after them. Make sure their every need is catered for; from getting water for the star, to setting up the next shot for the director. If you do this, they will love you, and you will get a reputation as an excellent researcher, one that everybody wants to work with. And when things go wrong, never, never get defensive – take the blame manfully, and get on with your job. Because here's the thing about being a researcher: it's always your fault!

Dealing with the crew

Know this: crews work very hard, for not a lot of money. Look after them too – bring them cups of coffee, and help carry the equipment. Just because it would be a nice thing to do . . .

The importance of time-code

If your production doesn't have a PA, you must learn how to take time-coded notes and mark up a script. Time-code is important; it helps your editor find the brilliant stuff that you shot. It's a message sent from the camera to the editing machine, by way of a series of numbers which are encoded onto the videotape. There are two types:

◆ tape-elapsed time-code

◆ and time-of-day time-code,

and the camera operator can set the camera to record either of them. Both types of TC have their advantages and disadvantages, but you'll probably find it easier to use time-of-day time code. Tape-elapsed TC is a record of the amount of tape that's been used in the shoot so far, which is a nice clear way of recording the information, but the disadvantage is that you have to read tape-elapsed TC off the side of the camera, or buy a special bit of equipment to read it remotely. Time-of-day TC is much simpler to use – you can read it off your watch – but the disadvantage is that the numbers can jump around (say, for instance, you finish shooting at 18.37, but you've only used half a tape. The next morning when you start shooting again, the time-code will jump from 18.37 to 08.15).

If this all sounds terribly complicated, don't worry – keeping time-of-day TC notes just means writing down a list of the time when you shot stuff. PAs make very clever notes, using jargon and special PA techniques, but you won't be expected to do that – as long as your notes are clear and easy to read, the editor will find them useful. Here are some things to know about taking basic time-code notes:

1. You'll need a good digital watch.

2. Always ask your camera operator to use time-of-day time code, and synchronise your watch with the camera before you start to shoot.

3. Every time the camera operator turns over, take a note of the time on your watch – to the second – and write down a brief description of the shot.

4. You need to know the names for the most common types of shot: BCU = big close up. CU = close up. MCU = medium close up. MS = mid shot. MLS = medium long

shot. LS = long shot. WS = wide shot. And the most common descriptions of shots: H/A = high angle. L/A = low angle. O/S = over-the-shoulder. POV = point of view. GVs = general views (a useful phrase when you're not sure exactly what the camera operator is shooting). PTC = piece to camera. C/A = cut away (something happening away from the main action). And so on.

Here's what a marked up script looks like:

PTC 1:
Tape 3:10.46.23, Take 4
(also look at take 2: 10.42.35)*
Take 1 n/g – camera
Take 3 n/g – sound

GLAMOROUS PRESENTER:
You might think that Porta Marina is an unusual place to come on your holidays...

O/S:
Tape 3: 10.57.12
C/As fishermen:
Tape 4: 11.03.16–11.22.17**

(CUT TO AN O/S SHOT TO SEE THAT SHE HAS TETHERED A FISHING BOAT. THE FISHERMEN ON BOARD WAVE THEIR THANKS. CUT TO TIGHTER SHOT OF PRESENTER)

PTC 2:
Tape 4: 12.40.57, Take 6
(also look at take 1: 12.20.34)
Take 2 n/g – words
Take 3 n/g – action
Take 4 n/g – camera
Take 5 n/g – performance

GLAMOROUS PRESENTER:
It's a working fishing port, and there's not a beach, or a water park, or a shopping mall, for miles around.

WS people eating:
Tape 6: 17.34.56 and 17.35.13
Singles people eating:
Tape 6: 17.55.10– 18.03.20
(good shots @ 17.56.40 and 18.01.12)

(CUT TO MONTAGE OF SHOTS AROUND TOWN – TOURISTS EATING, SHOPPING AND ENJOYING THEMSELVES. KIDS FISHING OFF PIER, KIDS WITH PARENTS ETC)

CU food, hands etc:
Tape 6: 17.40.33 – 17.44.20
(good shots @ 17. 41 (ish)
Good shots of kids with
parents:
Tape 4: 12.43.17
Shots of kids fishing off pier:
Tape 4: 13.01.13
Shopping GVS:
Tape 6: 18.28.02–18.38.45
(interesting shots @ 18.30
(ish)*** – nice looking people!

GLAMOROUS PRESENTER V/O:
But this is Portugal's new family holiday hotspot. Here's why . . .

The asterisks are there to highlight some important points about time code:

*The director kept going until Take 4, but you thought that Take 2 was worth looking at, perhaps because there was a nice boat in the background, or the presenter seemed more relaxed in this take – this is important information to tell the editor, so she can look at both takes and decide for herself. It's also helpful if you tell her what's wrong with the other PTCs (n/g means no good, because of camera problems, or performance, or the presenter fluffed the words, or whatever). As a rule, it's always helpful to note good shots, so the editor can make a point of looking out for them. This is easy to discern on a PTC because the director will say something like: 'Okay, let's go again,' or something else helpful like: 'Do it again please, but make it better this time.' And once you strike up a relationship with your camera operator, he will let you know the good shots, by slipping you the wink, or saying: 'That was a good shot.'

**The camera operator shot a lot of cut aways of fishermen. You don't need to detail all of them, just give the editor a rough idea of where the shots are.

***You weren't paying attention at this point, obviously – perhaps you'd gone to get the presenter a bottle of water – but when you got back, the camera operator said that the crew picked up some nice shots at around 6.30. Your notes don't need to be frame accurate – the editor will look at all the shots anyway – but your edit will run more smoothly (and *much* more quickly) if there's a record of roughly where all the shots are.

Doing interviews

On some programmes – mainly documentary programmes where there isn't a location presenter – researchers are expected to do the interviews on the stories they have set up. If you are asked to do an interview, don't be scared. An interview is just a conversation, and you have those every day. Once you've done a few, your interview techniques will become second nature. Until then, here are some things to bear in mind:

◆ Ask the obvious questions. Assume nothing. You may have been researching this story for weeks, but the viewer knows nothing about it.

◆ It's good to have a checklist of questions, but don't keep referring to it – look the interviewee straight in the eye and *listen* to what he or she is saying. If you're studying your list and thinking about your next question, you could miss something interesting; something that demands a follow-up question. If you do decide to use a checklist, don't write the question out in full – just use key words to jog your memory; you should retain eye contact with your interviewee for as long as you can.

◆ Don't ask questions that can be answered by a straight 'yes' or 'no'. Say things like: 'Tell me about your holiday that went horribly wrong.'

◆ Never, never, ever interrupt. Keep your mouth firmly closed until the interviewee has stopped speaking – don't even murmur an agreement or encouragement; nod and smile instead. The editor will find the piece impossible to edit if your voice keeps interjecting.

◆ If your interviewee is painfully shy, there's an old TV trick you can play on them to stop them seizing up: tell them that you're going to do a rehearsal of the interview, then record the rehearsal. Works wonders every time. (Be sure to warn the crew what you're doing though . . .) Unless you're going to play this trick on your hapless interviewee, I would caution you *not* to rehearse the interview, otherwise when you go to record for real, the interviewee will say things like: 'As I said before . . .', or even worse, they'll forget to tell an important part of the story because they thought they had already recorded that part of the interview. Try to keep your interviews spontaneous – they'll feel fresher.

Studio discipline and etiquette

If you are shooting in studio there are four things to remember:

1. In studio, the floor manager is king (well, actually, he's the manager, but you know what I mean). It may be your story, and your interviewee, but it is the floor manager's floor, and don't ever forget it. Always introduce your interviewees to the floor manager, and, if you want to stay on the studio floor, it's polite to ask the floor manager's permission. (It's also important from a health and safety point of view that the floor manager knows exactly who's in studio at any time.)

2. The studio is a scary place for a novice interviewee – much scarier than being interviewed on location. It's big, and full of bright lights, and TV professionals who've seen it all before and then some. If your contributor is a sensitive type, he may need extra TLC.

3. Never enter studio on a red light.

4. Never enter studio on a red light. This is worth saying twice because it's so important. If you screw up an otherwise perfect Take 20, everyone on the crew will hate you. Forever.

5. And never, ever, ever be late back from coffee break or lunch. Studio runs like a well-oiled machine. It's highly unprofessional – not to mention rude – to be late for studio. You don't want to keep 50 highly-paid people hanging around waiting for you. Trust me, you really don't.

POST-PRODUCTION

Editing

You may or may not get to see your programme through to post-production; depends on your contract. But if you get the chance, try to sit in on some editing – even if you have to do it in your own time. Editing is a fantastic process. It's supremely satisfying to see your ideas taking shape, and you can learn a lot from watching the editor: what works, what doesn't, and whether your time-code notes were any good or not!

Dubbing

You won't have to organise a dubbing session until you're a fairly senior researcher, but you may be asked to write voice-over scripts, to be recorded during your production's dubbing time. There are three golden rules to writing V/Os, or commentaries:

1. Don't write what you can see. It's tedious for the viewer if all your script does is describe what's happening on the screen – your words should *add* to the pictures. So if you're writing voice-over for a game-show where the contestants are racing over an assault course, don't say: 'And Tristram is running towards the rope swings.' Everybody watching the show will be able to see that he's running towards the rope swings, and they will be irritated to be told something so patently obvious. Much better to say something that the viewer doesn't know, like: 'Tristram needs to get a move on now – he's three seconds behind.'

2. Leave plenty of space. The basic rule for commentary writing is to allow three words per second. It's a good rule, as long as you also leave some *extra* space for the action to breathe, and for the pictures to speak for themselves. Wall-to-wall voice-over sounds terrible.

3. Keep it simple. Television is not a good medium for communicating complicated facts. Introduce one thought per sentence, then leave a gap so that the viewer can digest the thought.

The main reason people get commentary wrong is because they sit in the cutting room, watching a sequence over and over again, and it seems boring. So they 'liven it up', by adding voice-over. What they should really do, of course, is re-edit the sequence to make it less boring.

Clearing up

Don't worry, you don't have to tidy the office – this is the TV term for tying up all the loose ends at the end of a production. Three important things to remember at this stage:

◆ Make sure that the PA or production secretary has details of any music or archive you used in the programme, before you disappear off to work on a new project (see Chapter 9).

◆ File all your notebooks and contact lists from the programme. Throw nothing away – you may need to justify your research at a later date.

◆ And always, always write a nice thank-you letter to every
one of your contributors, letting them know when the
programme will be aired.

Finally, here are my five golden rules for having a happy
career as a researcher:

FIVE GOLDEN RULES FOR RESEARCHERS

1. Never be late. Whatever you're working on, turn up half
   an hour early, well prepared and ready for action.

2. Never say anything bad about anyone else's programme.
   Always find positive things to say. Remember that everyone sets out to make the best programme possible. So be
   kind. If you do feel you have to make a constructive
   comment, say something innocuous like: 'I wasn't sure
   about the presenter.' This is safe territory: nobody is ever
   sure about their presenter.

3. Always be free with your ideas, there are plenty more
   where they came from. The more ideas you give away,
   the more you'll have; your idea muscle will get bigger
   with practice.

4. Do *everything* with enthusiasm, no matter how big and
   important you think you are. A friend of mine joined the
   BBC as a studio cameraman. Six weeks into his career, he
   was told to clean the studio (a new floor had been laid,
   and the whole studio was thick with dust). So my friend
   cleaned the studio, meticulously and thoroughly, until it

was spotless and fit for making television programmes. For one afternoon, he was the best studio cleaner in the whole world. And that attitude has done him proud. He now runs his own department.

5. Always remember that television is a team sport – a programme is never made by just one person. So help and support everybody on the team, above, below and level with you. People who bitch and back-stab don't get asked back onto productions, no matter how good they are, because they're tedious to work with, and they can't be trusted.

7

Doing Any Other Job

This is not a technical manual, so we're not going to examine how to frame a shot, or edit a sequence, or count bars of music – anyway, these are skills you should be taught during your training. In this chapter, we're going to look at the most important skill you'll need to develop if you're going to make it in television – the skill of getting along with producers and directors. In fact, this chapter could be called 'What Producers and Directors Want'. Because here's the thing: if producers and directors like you, they will ask for you on their productions. If you work for a big company this is a good thing because you will become a valuable asset; the last person to get fired when times are hard. If you work as a freelance, it's an even better thing because producers and directors, and their production managers, will be queuing up to hire you, and you will always have work.

KNOWING WHAT PRODUCERS AND DIRECTORS WANT

To research this chapter, I interviewed producers and directors who, collectively, have worked on just about every type of television programme you can imagine. On your behalf, I asked them what they wanted from their crews, editors, unit managers and PAs, and they all said pretty much the same. Here's a summary of their ruminations, condensed into six simple rules.

1. Take things seriously, but not too seriously

Making television is a serious business. Even making comedy programmes is a serious business. If things go wrong, there are jobs at stake, and reputations, and lots and lots of money. So producers and directors want people who are dedicated, hardworking and professional. It's important that you're never late, and that you give every production your undivided concentration. But it's also important that you know how to have a laugh.

Here's a story: Richard is a producer/director with 30 years' experience. Recently he was shooting a drama with a tight schedule . . . and a dedicated, hardworking first assistant director who was severely lacking in the sense of humour department. He recalls the shoot with a shudder:

'She was obsessed with finishing every scene dead on schedule, and she took it as a personal affront if we fell even a few minutes behind. It's a big part of the first assistant director's job to drive the shoot, and keep an eye on the schedule, but she got things rather out of perspective. Every time we fell behind, she would start twitching and looking at her watch, and nagging the crew. Pretty soon, the atmosphere was awful – really tense and bad-natured – and the crew were getting more fed up by the minute. So I had to spend a lot of my time trying to lighten things, by cracking jokes and being jolly, but as soon as I got some goodwill going, she killed it stone dead with her attitude.'

For the record, he has vowed never to work with her again. Other producers and directors had similar stories of when good healthy professionalism goes bad, and slides into unhealthy neurosis.

2. Think about other people on the team

The big thing that marks out good people is that they always think about the whole process of making a television programme. They're aware of how their actions will affect other people's jobs, and they expend a lot of energy trying to help everybody else on the team (toadying to the people above you doesn't count, good people are nice to *everyone* – above, below and sideways!). A good camera operator goes to the edit when she gets a spare hour or two, because she understands that the more she knows about the editing process, the more she can do to help out her editor. A good editor will help a new researcher; show him the ropes and explain how editing works. Sometimes little gestures can make all the difference. All of the producers and directors I spoke to remembered small kindnesses, like the time when a PA brought out a giant bag of sweets on location and handed them round because there was no time for a coffee break. Being nice and kind and thoughtful will earn you a place in the affections of every producer and director you work with. Upsetting other people will do you no good at all, in fact in may do you a lot of harm – television is a democratic industry, and new recruits can rise quickly through the ranks. You never know who's going to be a producer next year.

Another cautionary tale: Brian was a brilliant but grumpy editor who took no prisoners, didn't suffer fools, and other polite ways of saying that he was a nasty piece of work. He hated greenhorns, and instead of helping fresh-faced young people, he'd shred them with his spiky tongue. One particular new recruit really got his goat, and he growled at him: 'Either you go back to your office and tell them you're rubbish, or I will!'. Imagine Brian's surprise when, 18 months later, that same young researcher turned up as the series producer on a new show that Brian was due to edit.

3. Be confident, but never dominate

I was talking to two directors about the most important quality in a camera operator/sound recordist/assistant direc-tor/PA/editor. 'Confidence,' said one. 'But not *too* much confidence,' said the other. The first director nodded in agreement. 'Please explain,' I said. Here's the gist of their explanation: you need to have an open, honest and frank exchange of views with your team, so your team should be made up of people who are confident in their own abilities. A chip on the shoulder is a very bad thing. A director should be able to say to his editor: 'that cut doesn't work', without worrying that he might upset her. Equally, an editor has to be able to say to her director: 'that shot has to go, even though you spent three hours setting it up . . .' A good camera operator has the confidence to interpret what the director wants, and the judgement to shoot it in the way that an editor can cut it. Sometimes there's no time to ask: 'is this what you want?' Confidence is important in every television job. But over-confidence can cause problems. Some people get carried away, and forget that they're not in charge of the shoot. This is bad.

Richard told the story of when he first started directing drama, and he was assigned a very experienced, very enthusiastic cameraman.

'He was forever suggesting ideas and brilliant shots, so I kept changing the shots I had planned to do. He was very persuasive. But when I got back to the edit. I couldn't cut any of the shots that he had suggested into the programme; they didn't go with the rest of the sequences I had so carefully planned. The problem was that he couldn't see the big picture – he was only working shot to shot – but I knew the story I wanted to tell. I'd been carrying it around in my head for weeks. I should have stuck to my guns. Now I always tell new directors: 'don't allow the camera operator to dominate . . .' The best camera operators feel that they have an equal relationship with you, but they defer to your understanding of the material. They never dominate.'

Gordon had a similar story to tell. He once worked with an overbearing cameraman who didn't just *suggest* new shots, he went right ahead and did them, regardless of what Gordon had asked for. Gordon had two options: to tackle the cocky cameraman himself – which could have provoked some unpleasantness – or to discuss the problem with the cameraman's manager. He chose the latter route. Big mistake. Next day on location, the cameraman was tight-lipped, and would only do *exactly* what Gordon requested, no suggestions, no enthusiasm and definitely no good. The remainder of the shoot was a very bad experience.

These two terrible stories should never have happened. Good people understand that no matter how brilliant their individual skills are, there is only one director, and the director always has the final say.

4. Respect everyone else

You know that you are good at your job. Assume everyone else is too. You will work with different groups of people every time you start a new production. Don't waste time sizing them up or being suspicious – things will run much more smoothly if you respect them all, no questions asked. And your director will love you for it. All directors complain about the 'fencing' that goes on when they first work with someone new – that first moment when a director meets his camera crew, and they parry and thrust to find out how much he knows, how much technical knowledge he has, and what

sort of programmes he's done before. Paul has been directing single-camera shoots for 20 years, and he still has to deal
with the fencing, every time he works with a new crew.
Here's his idea of a dream crew:

> 'We would meet, introduce each other, they would
> assume that I'm a competent guy, and everybody would
> get on with their work. Same goes for editors, unit
> managers, and PAs.'

It works both ways, though – directors have to learn to
respect their teams too, no questions asked.

A director friend of mine had to shoot for a week in
New York with an American crew he didn't know.
When he was introduced to the sound recordist, the
young man grasped his hand enthusiastically and
said: 'I'm really glad to get the chance to do this
shoot with you. Normally I'm a writer, but I need
some extra money for creative writing classes.' My
friend felt the colour drain from his face, and he
spent the whole shoot peering at the young man to
check that he really was recording some sound. He
needn't have worried – the sound was fine. He
should have trusted the cameraman who hired the
sound recordist, and the production manager who
hired the cameraman. They both had reputations to
keep up; they wouldn't risk their good names hiring a
no-good sound recordist.

5. Be a 'can do', not a 'can't do'

Never go to a producer or director with problems, unless you have some solutions. Producers and directors don't like working with people who say 'I can't do because . . .'. They're really not interested in the becauses – they expect you to sort out your own problems, and only come to them if there's a really major hitch that would jeopardise the programme, and they really, absolutely need to know about it. And even then, they expect you to come to them with some ideas on how to solve the problem. Here's Paul:

'Sometimes people like to tell you their problems, and how hard they've had to work to overcome them, just so they can underline how difficult their job is and win your approval. I hate that. I know everyone has a difficult job, but I don't want it dumped on me, especially when I'm under pressure. If you're producing and directing a programme, sometimes you feel as though all you do is deal with other people's problems – there's a line of problem-people outside your door. You deal with one, and then shout: "Next!". You don't have time to do any real work. Most problems should never reach the producer or director. I like working with problem-solvers, not problem-givers.'

6. Expect to suffer for your art

There's an old joke that goes something like this: a circus comes to town, and right at the end of the procession, there's a chap whose job it is to shovel up the elephant muck, and put it in a bucket. A kindly old lady is watching him scooping up the dirt, and she says: 'Young man, why don't you get another job?', and the man stands up, looks at her dumb-

founded and says: 'What, and give up show business!' Sometimes television can get like that – not elephant dung,
exactly, but I have friends who have worked a 12 hour day in
sub-zero conditions. And then they've gone back the next
day and done another 12 hours in sub-zero conditions. And
the same the next day, and the next . . . And then they've
gone straight into a night shoot. You have to love your job,
really love it, if you want to be happy in television.

Expect to work very long hours, in difficult working conditions. Expect to be sunburned, heat-fatigued, mosquito-
bitten, frostbitten, and even moth-eaten, but don't expect a
nice cushy job. And expect to put your social life second to
the production – schedules can change suddenly, and your
weekend plans may have to be shelved at short notice. It's
become such a cliché to say: 'Oh, my job *seems* glamorous,
but it's really very hard work . . .'. Models say this in
interviews, meaning that they had to walk up and down a
few extra times, or change their clothes quite quickly, or
maybe go to three parties *in one night!* But television really
is hard work, sometimes grindingly hard work, and only the
fittest, the most enthusiastic and the most focused people
survive.

And that's the secret of television. If you can do your
job well, and you follow these six simple rules, you
are guaranteed a good reputation and a glittering career.
Promise.

Part 4
Things You Should Know

'To get into this industry, you need to know your subject. Do stacks of research.'

Emma Clifford, Training & Development Manager, ITV News Group

$$\boxed{8}$$

Rules and Regulations

Television is the most heavily regulated industry in the world. Apart from nuclear power. And the railways. And industrial chemicals. Oh, and airlines.

The rules and regulations that you must obey when you make a programme fall into three categories:

◆ criminal law

◆ civil law

◆ and the various broadcasting codes and standards.

CRIMINAL LAW

Obviously, you shouldn't commit any criminal acts in order to make a television programme. Easy to say, but it's not quite as simple as that – at some point in your television career you may well be faced with decisions that take you onto the fringes of criminal activity.

True story: a famous BBC presenter went out to shoot some vox pops interviews, and ended up getting herself arrested. She was filming for her consumer programme in a busy London street. A small crowd had gathered, and a passing policeman decided that they were causing an obstruction. He asked the crew to move on. Now the sensible thing to do would have been to go round the corner, and come back later. But the presenter was a champion of people's rights, so she decided to make an issue of it. So the policeman arrested her.

Moral: if you're going to stand your ground on an issue, you need to be very, very sure that you know what you're talking about. There is no specific law in Britain that says you can't film in a public place, but there are lots of grey areas within the law that mean the police can stop you if they really want to – especially if you start to argue with them.

Another grey area is the idea of 'public interest'. Say you're working on a documentary piece about how easy it is to smuggle weapons onto an aircraft. You might be justified in trying it yourself, in order to get dramatic visual evidence of just how lax airport security is. But there's a huge risk involved because you'd be breaking the law. Such a sequence would need to be approved in advance by a very senior executive from the production company. And cleared by the broadcaster. And checked by legal experts. And you could still end up going to prison.

If you're doing any sort of story involving courts and the legal system, warning bells should ring in your head. There are restrictions on discussing on-going trials, which can have serious criminal penalties. The details are beyond the scope of this book, but beware of dabbling in legal stories unless you're absolutely sure of the rules.

Breaking health and safety regulations can also incur criminal penalties – see Chapter 9 for details:

CIVIL LAW

The three areas to be aware of are:

◆ defamation

◆ trespass

◆ copyright.

DEFAMATION

Libel is defamation published in permanent form. Slander is defamation by unrecorded speech or gesture. In the UK, broadcasting is regarded as publication in permanent form, so broadcast defamation is libel. British law aims to protect the reputation of individuals, while at the same time allowing free speech and fair comment. The key test – for both the court and the producer – is: does this statement cause quantifiable damage to the individual? If you say (or imply) in a comedy show that the Prime Minister wears funny pyjamas, it's not defamation because it doesn't cause any damage to his reputation. But if you say (or imply) that an actor is gay, prepare to get sued. Even in the twenty-first century it can be libellous to say that someone is not heterosexual.

It's possible to libel someone quite by accident. A regional journalist was once putting together a story about the trial of two police officers who'd been doing something illegal – to protect the innocent, let's say claiming fraudulent expenses. He didn't have any pictures of them arriving at court, so he used some library shots of the court building. By a stroke of horrible bad luck, there were two completely different policemen in the library shots. They claimed that the item was libellous, as it could have led people to assume that they were the accused. The courts agreed, and it cost the TV company a bundle of money.

TRESPASS, LOCATION FEES AND FILMING PERMITS

Anyone who enters private property without permission is trespassing. But trespass that causes no damage is not a criminal offence in Britain – so those notices that say *'trespassers will be prosecuted'* are bluffing. But the property owner can sue a trespasser, so it's important to get permission before filming on private land. Once the property owner has given permission, he may well ask you to pay a location fee.

If you're filming abroad, be aware that you may need a filming permit, even to film in a public area. And if you're filming in America, assume that you will need one, especially if you're filming in a city (check by phoning the Mayor's office). The city of LA is the worst place in the world for filming permits. It's a city that makes its living out of filming, and they have an entire office set up to take money from film-makers, no matter how big or small. You need a permit for every set-up: that'll be several hundred dollars, please, for the 20-second PTC on a Hollywood sidewalk; and another several hundred for the walking shot on Venice Beach. We shot a story in an LA flood channel, but unfortunately the bit of flood channel we wanted to use was owned by two different authorities – the City of Los Angeles, and the Corps of Engineers – so we had to buy two separate permits, at a cost of almost a thousand dollars. All for two hours of filming.

That's the bad news. The good news is that once you've bought your permit you will appear on the city's daily 'Shoot Sheet', a list of all the productions shooting anywhere in LA that day – so you could find yourself billed next to Steven Spielberg!

(A confession: for budgetary reasons, I have sometimes filmed without a permit, grabbing shots on the run, just one step ahead of the law. It sounds romantic and thrilling, but in reality it's terrifying, and very bad for your blood pressure. I could never officially advise you to film without a permit in areas where one is required – if you do, the police have the right to stop the shoot, which would be catastrophic if you were on a tight schedule.)

COPYRIGHT

Every clip of a movie, every photograph, every snippet of archive film, every bit of artwork, and every piece of music is owned by someone. And if you want to use it in your programme, you have to pay for it. Once you enter the area of copyright, you need to tread carefully; it's a minefield. Here are the danger areas.

Music

Music always costs money. Every bit of music you use in a programme must be logged in detail (title, writer, publisher and recording artist) and paid for, whether it's a recording of a live band, or just a snatch from a CD.

Here's a cheap and cheerful guide – but *always* check with an expert. (Or at least send an e-mail to someone higher up than you so that they'll get the blame if it goes wrong . . .)

Suppose you want to cut a montage to a commercially available track. You've got the CD in your hand, but that doesn't mean you can use it, because the copyright is owned by up to three people or organisations:

◆ First, there's a copyright in the **Musical Work** itself, which is owned by the composer. It's often assigned to a music publisher who collects the fees on the composer's behalf; and it lasts for 70 years after the death of the composer.

◆ Next is the copyright in the **Sound Recording,** normally held by the record company for 50 years from the date the recording was first issued.

◆ Finally there's a copyright in the **Performance,** initially owned by the musicians and singers. But normally these rights are assigned to, and dealt with, by the record company, so needn't trouble us now.

British law gives the copyright holder the exclusive right to do certain things with the material:

◆ to copy it

◆ to issue copies to the public

◆ to perform it in public

◆ to broadcast it

◆ to adapt it

◆ finally to rent or lend it to the public.

Only two of these rights are exercised during the making of a TV programme: when the music is copied (for example when you transfer it from the CD to the magnetic storage on your editing system); and when the music is broadcast as part of a TV programme. To do this legally, you have to pay a fee to the copyright holders.

The money in both cases is collected by various copyright societies, which in turn distribute the money to the rights holders. With me so far?

1. So first, the copying right. This is collected by an organisation called MCPS – the Mechanical Copyright Protection Society. Most big TV companies have a

blanket agreement, and pay a huge chunk of money each year. Individual producers are responsible for reporting what music they've used to the music department, who in turn report to MCPS. MCPS then pays out the money to the rights holders. (Note that if you were making a programme as a completely independent producer, you'd need to join MCPS, and pay on a track by track basis.)

2. Next the performing right. The broadcaster pays this – Channel 4, the BBC, whoever – and again, all the companies have blanket agreements. The money in this case is collected by the PRS (Performing Rights Society) and distributed to the rights holders in a similar way to MCPS.

3. Finally the right to use a particular commercial recording is granted by an organisation called the BPI (the British Phonographic Industry). And guess what – most big companies have a blanket agreement that covers use in a UK programme. However, if your programme is likely to be sold overseas, you must get advance clearance from the record company. Many tracks aren't clearable for foreign sales, including, for example, anything by The Beatles.

Knowing what you can use
So, enough legal talk. How does this affect you and your programme?

◆ First, you can always clear live performances, of any piece of music, as long as you're working under the MCPS blanket agreement. The only exception is where the performance is 'abnormal' – which means anything that the rights holder might object to. So your presenter humming 'New York, New York' in a yellow cab in Manhattan is fine, but having her sing different words to the same tune would be abnormal, and would need advance clearance. Another example of abnormal use would be using a piece of music over a disturbing scene in a drama – like a violent attack, or a suicide attempt. The rule is: any straight performance is OK; anything else should be checked in advance.

◆ The safest music to use is from library discs; they are always clearable. There are thousands of them, called things like 'Comedy Themes' and 'News Punctuation'. There are some very good tracks, and some absolutely dire ones. So you'll need to listen to a lot to find the one that's just right for your piece.

◆ Equally safe, but rather more expensive, is to have the music specially composed, because the clearances required can be specified in the contract with the composer.

◆ Commercial records can be used (though not normally as title music). Most big UK record companies are signatories to the BPI agreement, so a UK artist on a big label should present no problems for a UK programme. If you want to use an artist on a small indie label, you'll almost certainly need up-front clearance and to pay a fee. And as noted above, you always need special clearance to use a commercial record on a programme that is to be sold abroad.

Finally, it's worth knowing that there are different rates for the various ways music is used in a programme.

◆ If the music is added afterwards – as when you cut a montage – then it's called 'incidental' music.

◆ If the participants in the scene can hear the music then it's called 'featured' music – for example a family in a drama with a radio playing in the background. (Note that this is a totally theoretical distinction, since virtually all TV music is in fact added afterwards, for technical reasons. If you record dialogue with music playing, you can't edit the dialogue without the music jumping.)

◆ And finally there's 'actuality' – which is when you record the musicians playing live.

That's it, except to say this: if in doubt, check. Mistakes can be expensive!

Archive

There are plenty of specialist companies dealing in archive film and photographs, and as a rule they charge plenty of money for their services. Bear in mind there's a copyright fee to pay *every time* a piece of archive gets shown, and costs vary depending on whether transmission is world-wide, national or regional. Always check costs before you order any archive, and get a quote in writing. And it's always worth trying to negotiate a better price. Sometimes you need to use quite a bit of archive – if you're making a historical piece, for instance – and one way to keep costs down is to get the material from source. Years ago, I wrote a story about skyscrapers in New York which went into great detail about the invention of elevators. I called the New York Historical Society to discuss getting photographs to illustrate the piece, but the cost was prohibitive – hundreds of dollars for prints and copyright use, which our budget just couldn't cover. So I called the company founded by the man who invented elevators: the Otis Elevator Company in Connecticut, who have their very own archivist, and a whole store of wonderful photographs and film from the turn of the century. The film showed skyscrapers being built, early lifts being tested, and some brilliant shots of the New York skyline as it developed. And do you know the best thing – they gave us free use, because they liked the story!

Movies
Even a short clip of a feature film will cost you thousands of pounds, unless your transmission falls within the 'free use window'. This is a period of a few weeks either side of the movie's release, in cinemas or on video, when you get free use because the film is being promoted – so no problem for a movie magazine show reviewing the latest releases. If you need a clip for another reason – say you're doing a story looking at the new digital technology used to produce film special effects – always check the length of the free use window; it varies from company to company. And always get a contract clearly stating the terms of your agreement. Review programmes are a great way of getting free material. We once made a computer games magazine show for £2,000 for a ten-minute programme (astonishingly cheap pro-gramming in 1996!). It consisted of one presenter, a couple of game-players, and an endless supply of free-use computer games material.

BROADCASTING CODES AND STANDARDS

All broadcasters in the UK have to follow guidelines laid down by Office of Communications (Ofcom), who publish them in a book called the 'Programme Code'. The BBC is still partially regulated by its Board of Governors, and the rules are incorporated in its charter.

The Programme Code covers areas like: fairness, taste and decency; the portrayal of violence; privacy and the gathering of information; dealing with the police and the law; and responding to viewers.

One important bit to be aware of is the area of product placement and sponsorship. The guidelines state that there mustn't be 'undue prominence' for commercial products. So it's probably okay to get a free flight with British Airways, and, as part of the story, show one shot of a plane with the BA logo on its tail. In this instance, the plane features as part of the story, so the use is not 'undue' and if you only use one quick shot of a plane's tail logo, it's not too 'prominent' either. But it's probably not okay to do an entire item about hi-fi products that features the Sony logo in every close up. There are lots of hi-fi manufacturers, so just featuring Sony products is certainly undue and definitely more prominent than necessary.

Product placement has a specific meaning – it's where a company pays money to have its product featured. Common in movies, and on American TV; completely outlawed in the UK.

It's worth getting hold of various codes, and reading them thoroughly (Ofcom's website has details of how to order a copy of the Programme Code). The truth is that lots of TV people have only a vague idea about the rules – you could make yourself indispensable (and very popular) by becoming an expert!

9

Health and Safety

Whatever job you do, you need to know about health and safety. In most companies a health and safety form has to be completed for every shoot, no matter how big or small, assessing all the risks, no matter how big or small. The forms are detailed, and there's a lot of technical stuff that you need to know about doing risk assessment, which you'll learn on the job. But the whole issue of health and safety is really quite simple, as long as you use your common sense. The big thing to remember is: no shot is worth getting somebody injured for.

A HEALTH AND SAFETY QUIZ

So, with that thought in mind, it's quiz time again. (Oh good, we haven't had one since Chapter 2!) Imagine this: you're about to do a shoot in Florida. It's for a children's programme, so the presenter – let's call her Candy – will be getting involved, taking part in all sorts of exciting activities. Here are the five stories that you'll be shooting over your five days in Florida.

1. Candy learns to windsurf. She'll be taught by a member of the American Olympic windsurfing team. And

although Candy's never done anything like this before, we're promised that she'll be able to sail on the open ocean by the end of the afternoon.

2. Candy goes into the Everglades with an alligator hunter, who says that Candy will be able to help him quite a lot, as it takes two people to hold down a fully grown gator . . .

3. Candy takes part in a rodeo. She can ride – according to her agent – so we've arranged for her to have a go at calf roping. And maybe steer wrestling. And perhaps a little light bull riding . . .

4. Candy visits a facility called Working Wildlife, a place were they train animals for the movies. They've got everything, apparently: grizzly bears, lions, tigers, wolves . . .

5. The highlight of the week: Candy gets to fly a fighter plane and have a dogfight. It's a tourist thing, but the planes are real fighter trainers. The guns are replaced by lasers, and each plane has a detector. When you get a hit, the opposing plane starts to stream smoke from its tail. Brilliant!

So, here's the quiz. Assess the risks of the whole shoot, and decide: what's the most dangerous thing you'll do all week?

Don't look in the box below to see the answer until you've made a decision!

The correct answer is that the most dangerous thing you'll do all week is . . .

. . . drive to and from location every day.

Surprised? The problem with risk assessment is that it's very difficult for an individual to consider risk logically. We're all influenced by preconceptions and emotional responses. Intuitively it seems that riding in a rodeo must be more dangerous than driving, but statistically you're far more likely to be killed or seriously injured in a car accident, especially when you're driving on the wrong side of the road (remember, we're in Florida!), and you're tired after a hard day's work.

Taking the examples one by one, let's consider the risks. (By the way, I've shot all these items for programmes, although admittedly not in a single week!)

Monday, Candy learns to windsurf

First, check she can swim. Sounds obvious, but the obvious is often overlooked. And don't just take the agent's word for it – they'll always say yes – but insist on speaking to the presenter direct, and make sure she knows exactly what you're planning.

When we shot this item, the presenter learned in a sheltered, shallow marina, with no waves. About as safe as we could make it. Then we moved to a bay known locally as 'Hurricane Gulch', where things were a bit choppier! The presenter didn't want to do it, and our instant risk assessment was that it was too dangerous. So we changed our minds – much to the presenter's relief – and thought up a different ending to the story. And that's lesson number one about health and safety: never be afraid to change your mind. If you're not happy about the safety of a sequence, just say no! In British law, every individual at work is responsible for their own safety, and the safety of their workmates. It's a criminal offence to be negligent – which means that if an accident happens and it's proved to be your fault, you can be fined or sent to prison. So don't take chances.

Tuesday, Candy goes gator hunting

Bobby the alligator hunter used to be an alligator poacher. Now he works for the Florida Wildlife Commission, catching and disposing of 'nuisance alligators'; ones that have had the temerity to stray close to people. He's survived into his sixties, and he still has all his limbs and other extremities, so he obviously understands gators. When we shot this story for real, we made sure that the crew had a proper briefing from Bobby first thing in the morning, so that everyone knew what to do if an alligator went for them. (For the record, in case it ever happens to you: you run in a zig-zag. Gators can outrun a human, but only in a straight line, and they're very stupid and easily confused.) Note that we arranged the briefing *before* the shoot started, so that we had time to pay attention to what Bobby had to say, without having to worry about shots, sound, scripts or schedule. I also made sure that the call sheet specified that everyone should wear long-sleeved shirts and trousers rather than shorts, to protect against insects. And I bought a plentiful supply of rhino strength bug spray. In fact the cameraman was the only one on the crew who came close to being in an unsafe position that day. He got a bit too close to an alligator he was taping, probably because he was looking through the viewfinder, which isolated him from the reality of the experience. (Danger, objects in the viewfinder are closer than they appear!). He got a fright when the gator suddenly lunged at him. After that, he retreated to a safer filming position, and used a longer lens . . .

So lesson two: do your utmost to ensure that everyone knows and understands the safety precautions, and has time to absorb the information.

Wednesday, Candy rides the rodeo

We shot this story at one of the top rodeos in the USA, so they didn't want to soil their reputation with any nasty accidents. The presenter we used was a good rider, plus we insisted that she wear full safety gear: helmet, pads and gloves. Then on the day we decided to have the presenter only do an event called 'goat tying', which is how children start learning rodeo skills. There was still a chance that she might fall off, so we also checked that there was an ambulance and paramedics on hand (they were there for the real rodeo later). This is an example of an intrinsically dangerous activity that we made as safe as possible by putting 'control measures' in place. And it made a great item!

So lesson three is: just because something is dangerous, it doesn't mean you can't do it. But you must make sure that you've thought about all the things that might go wrong, and what control measures are needed. And always shoot with the best people – experts who know what they're doing.

Thursday, Candy visits Working Wildlife

For the sake of the quiz, I moved this place to Florida from its real location in Los Angeles. Working Wildlife is where they train big, dangerous animals for movies. As the animal trainers got to know us, they started to offer more and more exciting things for us to do. Including: would we like our presenter to go for a walk with the lion? What would you say? The director and cameraman loved the idea. The presenter was less happy, and Tim the sound recordist wondered if, talking about danger, there was any danger of a tea break?

The director and I conferred and did an instant risk assessment. It went something like this:

Me: 'Are you sure it'll be safe?'

Him: 'Yeah . . .'

Me: 'I suppose their whole business revolves around animals being safe with stars . . .'

Him: 'Right, let's do it!'

Me: 'And they told me that the lion was hand reared, and is very calm with people . . .'

Him: 'It'll look fantastic with the mountains in the background.'

Me: 'And the handler will have the lion on a choke chain all the time.'

Him: 'Where did Tim get that cup of tea from?'

Well, you get the idea. It seemed to both of us that it would be a great shot, and the trainers wouldn't have offered it if it wasn't safe – their reputation relies on people *not* getting eaten by their lions! But as a precaution, I scribbled some safety notes down on the back of my copy of the call sheet – just to prove, if I ever needed to, that I had spent some time thinking about the risks. What happened next was interesting: the presenter was still scared, so I volunteered to have a go first, just to prove it was safe. The presenter agreed that if I didn't get eaten, then she'd have a go too. And she did, and it made a great sequence. (Later on the same day a leopard went mad and ate Tim's microphone – but that's another story . . .)

Lesson four: make sure you assess *every* activity for risks – even if it's something set up at the last minute. And make sure you make a note of your assessment in writing. Just in case, your honour . . .

Friday, Candy gets to fly a fighter plane and have a dogfight

The key here is that it's a tourist attraction. Licensed, reputable and obviously safe – they take people up every day. So the only real safety question is: are we adding to the risks by taping? The planes were two seaters, so the crew couldn't go up. So we shot this item by putting a minicam in the cockpit, with a cable running to a video recorder under one of the seats. We made sure that the pilot checked and approved the cable runs, and the positions of the camera and recorder. We also allowed plenty of time for the rig, so it could be done calmly and quietly. In fact on this particular day, 'health' was more of an issue than 'safety' – the presenter was violently airsick. She pleaded with us not to show the footage of her throwing up . . . but of course we did!

So lesson five is: make sure that the shooting doesn't make a safe activity dangerous. Be particularly aware of things like:

◆ cameras getting in the way in confined spaces such as cockpits of aircraft

◆ people concentrating on the filming instead of the activity

◆ and worst of all, people playing up to camera.

Years ago a well-known animal show did an item called 'the world's most poisonous snakes', and they had 12 of the nastiest ones in the studio. They recorded the item, making great play of the doctor and nurse on standby just behind the cameras. Then the studio was cleared, leaving just the item producer and the handler to put the snakes away. But – and here's the dangerous bit – the crew all gathered in the scene dock to watch the handler at work. He put away the most dangerous snakes first, carefully and methodically. But when he came to bag the swamp viper, he started playing to the crowd . . . and the snake whipped round and plunged its fangs into his hand. With great presence of mind, the handler put the snake into its bag – and then collapsed onto the studio floor. Of course by this time the doctor and nurse had left the studio, and gone for their tea break. The handler was rushed to hospital by ambulance, given the antidote, and he lived to tell the tale – with a painful arm for a few months to remind him not to play to the gallery.

The production team were at fault though, for allowing the crew to watch. Boring though it is, they should have insisted on giving the handler time and space to do his job without distractions.

We've had a quiz; now it's time for a riddle: when is a farmyard cow more dangerous than a charging steer? Give up? Well, do you remember cameraman Matt's dilemma back in Chapter 1: should he do the shot where the dangerous steer charges straight towards camera, and the cowboy lassoes the beast just before it reaches Matt? Of course, he decided to do it, for three reasons: firstly, he'd worked with the cowboy all day, and he trusted him. Secondly, the cowboy was a national rodeo champion, and he had a reputation to keep up. And thirdly, it made a fantastic shot. So the charging steer was relatively safe. Which is more than can be said for the placid dairy cow which had a bit part in a period drama. Picture the location set: it was a Victorian street scene, nicely cobbled and a bit mucky, with chickens, dogs, cows and a crowd of peasants all milling about in a pleasing Victorian fashion. What happened next surprised everyone. It was like a children's rhyme: the chicken clucked, which made the dog bark, which spooked the cow, so it skidded on the mucky cobbles, which caused the crowd to lunge backwards. And the poor peasant-woman extra right at the back of the surging crowd got a broken pelvis. Which just goes to show that no matter how much you think about safety, some risks just can't be anticipated.

CHECKING WHAT'S IMPORTANT

To sum up, here are five important things to remember about health and safety:

◆ No shot, for any television programme, is so important that it's worth somebody getting killed or injured for it.

◆ Everyone is responsible for everyone else's safety, and you could face a hefty fine – or even a prison sentence – if you do cause someone to be injured.

◆ The most common cause of accidents and near misses in the television industry is falling or tripping over cables and other objects – *not* being eaten by lions or crushed by a charging steer.

◆ Because the most dangerous thing you'll do all day is drive to location, always allow people plenty of time to get there. It's rushing that causes accidents.

◆ You can do just about anything, as long as you employ good control measures.

And Finally

Ever since television was invented in the 1930s, people have been predicting its downfall. The industry runs in cycles, sometimes triggered by technology; more often by social and economic considerations.

At the time of writing, the industry is in the doldrums. Despite the promise of digital, the vast expansion of available channels, and the coming of widescreen, the TV companies seem unable to make enough money. And once again the doom-sayers are out in force, with their rallying cry: 'The golden age of television ended a week ago last Thursday . . .'

Don't listen to them. The truth is that TV programmes are here to stay. The delivery systems may change. Audiences may be fragmented. And using advertising to fund channels may disappear as a business model. But people still want to be entertained, informed and educated by that small, colourful and exciting box in the corner.

WHAT THE FUTURE LOOKS LIKE

For what it's worth, here's my prediction: the high-end shows (expensive comedy and drama, often co-productions or American-made) will always be with us. They'll probably become 'pay-per-view', which means that instead of being broadcast on a free-to-air channel, you'll choose to watch them. In the future, we won't come home from work or school and say 'what's on TV tonight?' – we'll watch what we want to watch, when we want to watch it. Soaps will continue, at least in the short-term; they offer an escape into a safe and familiar world, so people become addicted to them. They're already the mainstay of ITV, and they almost guarantee an audience for free-to-air channels. The problem will be how to fund them: see below.

There's also a big future for very low-end, niche programming. If you can make a show for (say) boating enthusiasts, for a reasonable budget, then its audience will find it. Entire channels already work on this model (like *Discovery Wings*). There are lots of funding options as well – sponsorship being the obvious one. But this kind of niche audience will also be prepared to keep watching through the commercial break, because the adverts will be targeted and relevant.

And of course there will always be live, topical programmes: sport, news, current affairs, quizzes that give away a million dollars...

So where's the bad news?

I'm afraid there is some. The idea that an entire channel can be funded by advertising has had its day. The beginning of the end came with the remote control. The end of the end will be when a computer in your television can edit out the adverts, even when you're watching a live programme.

The new model will be sponsorship and product placement, so that the commercial messages are embedded in the content of the show itself. You can't watch the show without watching the advert . . .

Twenty years ago it was a given that the audiences were loyal to a channel. Some viewers watched BBC1 all evening; others were 'ITV types'. And a select few chose programmes on BBC2 or Channel 4. (In those days, BBC1 was perceived to have an advantage because it came up as the first button on most TV sets!) Today the audiences don't care what channel they're watching – hence the ubiquitous branding buttons in the top corner of the picture. People watch programmes rather than channels; fans of *Friends* will find reruns, wherever they are in the 200 channel EPG.

The programmes that will be hit hardest are the ones that you find in 'shoulder-peak' (as it's called) on terrestrial channels: shows that people watch when they come on, but probably wouldn't go out of their way to find. So cheap game shows are in danger, and bad docusoaps . . . in fact any general audience shows that aren't spectacularly successful.

YOUR FUTURE

But the good news is that the industry will *always* need content – and content comes from people like you. It's your ideas that are needed to take television forward. It's your enthusiasm and commitment that will create the most talked about shows next year, and five years from now. So, have a great career, in the best job in the world!

Index

If you want to know how . . . to be prepared for job interviews

'This book will take you through the essentials of preparing for an interview. Whether it is your first or your first in a long time – or even if you are an 'old hand' – you will find hints for success. Preparing to give a good performance, or at least giving your best, is what can guarantee success. You can tip the scales in your favour, with a little work beforehand.'

Julie-Ann Amos

Be Prepared!
Getting ready for job interviews
Julie-Ann Amos

'. . . succeeds in its aim of giving people the confidence to do well at an interview . . . a welcome addition to any careers library.' – *Newscheck*

'. . . easy to dip into and full of useful tips.' – *Phoenix Magazine*

A book that will give you the confidence to succeed at any interview – it covers everything from researching the company you're applying to work with to the golden rules of body language and how to handle nerves.

ISBN 1 85703 946 7

If you want to know how . . . to get a job in the film or television industry

'The future of films and television depends to a very great extent on the talent, training and commitment of new entrants.

'Robert Angell has, over the years, given advice to literally thousands of young people wanting to 'get into film or television'. In this book he consolidates that advice based on his many years as a documentary producer who started in the cutting room and progressed through many different areas of production.

'His book is both timely and welcome, and I'm certain it will prove useful to future generations of professionals in an industry to which Bob and I have devoted our lives with almost manic obsession.'

From the Foreword by David Puttnam
(Lord Puttnam, OBE)

Getting into Films and Television
Robert Angell

'The book will make an added contribution over and above the factual information about the real nature of working in the audio-visual industry. Highly recommended.'
– *ScriptWriter*

'A really useful guide to the subject.' – *The Daily Telegraph*

'This is an excellent publication . . . includes some real nuggets of information. The user-friendly print and layout ensure that even small items of advice or information are unlikely to be overlooked.' – *Newscheck*

ISBN 1 85703 974 2

If you want to know how . . . to handle tough job interviews

'Job interviews can be daunting, because often there is our livelihood at stake. A little preparation and understanding about how interviews work can help. Even better is understanding the purpose of the different stages of interview in a recruitment process, and the balance of power in those interviews.

'This book is about understanding why you are there, and what to do when things get difficult. It's about knowing your way through the recruitment process so that each hurdle is cleared to get you the job you want – if it's right for you.'

Julie-Ann Amos

Handling Tough Job Interviews
Be prepared, perform well, get the job
Julie-Ann Amos

'A wealth of sound advice.'
– *Sesame (Open University magazine)*

'Takes you step-by-step through the recruitment process and gives useful advice on interviews with senior management, dealing with psychometric tests; and discussing and agreeing the job offer.' – *Office Secretary*

'Its strength is that it covers all kinds of interview from recruitment agencies and headhunters to employer and human resources.' – *Phoenix Magazine*

ISBN 1 85703 845 2

If you want to know how . . . to pass psychometric tests

Over 95% of FTSE 100 companies use psychometric testing to select their staff; as do the police, the Civil Service, local authorities, the Armed Forces, the Fire Service, financial institutions, retail companies, the communications industry, the motor industry, the power industry – the list is endless. In fact, the vast majority of large–medium sized organisations use psychometric tests to recruit. So if you're looking for a job you need to know what to expect. This book gives you the information, confidence and practice to do that, and more.

Passing Psychometric Tests
Know what to expect and get the job you want
Andrea Shavick

'An insightful book.' – *The Guardian*

'A very good aid for those who might find themselves facing a psychometric questionnaire.' – *Irish Examiner*

ISBN 1 85703 819 3

If you want to know how . . . to prepare for interviews

'It's the interviewer's prerogative to throw just about any question they can think of at the interviewee. So you might think that it's almost impossible to prepare for an interview. But the truth is that 80% of interview questions revolve around 20 common themes. And many interviewees let themselves down by not thinking about these themes, preparing and rehearsing responses to them.

'Many candidates then go on to create a wrong impression. Remember that an interviewer has to *like* you and warm to you as a person, as well as want to work with you because you answer the questions well. I see too many candidates who talk too much or come across as nervous or unfriendly. If you get the chance to rehearse with a friend and get some feedback on just how you come across, you will improve your chances no end.'

Rob Yeung

Successful Interviews – Every Time
Rob Yeung

'*Successful Interviews* is the type of book that one may not wish to share with others who are job seeking in competition with oneself. Nevertheless, I owe a debt of gratitude to Dr Rob Yeung for sharing his experiences with us . . .'
– *S. Lewis, Coventry*

'This book is an invaluable source of information for job hunters on preparing for interviews, tests and assessment centres.' – *Jonathan Turpin, Chief Executive of job hunting website fish4jobs.co.uk*

ISBN 1 85703 978 5

If you want to know how . . . to find a
career in the world of music

'The music industry is a place you'll find excitement,
glamour, fun, creativity and passion. But be warned, you'll
also find exhaustion, frustration, swollen egos, depression,
poor pay and buckets of stress. You may know exactly what
kind of job you want and how to get it – good for you.
However, even those who think they know what a job in the
'music biz' entails, and feel they are up to the challenge,
can't lay their hands on much practical information on how
to break into what is a highly competitive field, and what to
expect when you're there.

This book is for you whether you intend to become chairman
of Sony Music or the roadie of choice for you favourite local
band! It aims to be brutally honest, realistic, practical and
full of insider secrets.'

Anna Britten

Working in the Music Industry
How to find an exciting and varied career in the world of
music
Anna Britten

Working in the Music Industry aims to help you take your
first step into what will be a long and satisfying career. Each
chapter covers a field of work within the music industry
– from record companies to recording studios to roadies –
and is crammed with honest, realistic, practical and helpful
advice. Insider secrets and individual case studies throw even
more light onto the subject.

'. . . a practical guide to realising your dreams in the music
industry.' – *Music Week*

ISBN 1 85703 974 2

How To Books are available through all good bookshops, or you can order direct from us through Grantham Book Services.

Tel: +44 (0)1476 541080
Fax: +44 (0)1476 541061
Email: orders@gbs.tbs-ltd.co.uk

Or via our website

www.howtobooks.co.uk

To order via any of these methods please quote the title(s) of the book(s) and your credit card number together with its expiry date.

For further information about our books and catalogue, please contact:

How To Books
3 Newtec Place
Magdalen Road
Oxford OX4 1RE

Visit our web site at

www.howtobooks.co.uk

Or you can contact us by email at info@howtobooks.co.uk